The Analects of Confucius

Translation and Notes by

SIMON LEYS

For information about permission to reproduce selections from this book,
write to Permissions, W. W. Norton & Company, Inc., 500 Fifth Avenue,
New York, NY 10110.

*Title page: Seal (in the personal use of the translator) "Wu yong Tang" ("Hall of
Uselessness"). This is a reference to Zhuang Zi: "People all understand the usefulness
of what is useful, but they do not understand the usefulness of what is useless."*

---

*The text of this book is composed in Monotype Bell
with the display set in Bauer Bodoni
Composition and Manufacturing by The Maple-Vail Book
Manufacturing Group
Book design by Antonina Krass*

Library of Congress Cataloging-in-Publication Data
Confucius.
[Lun yü. English]
The Analects of Confucius / translation and notes by Simon Leys.
p.   cm.
Includes bibliographical references and index.
ISBN 0-393-04019-4
I. Title.
PL2478.C57   1997
181'.112—dc20   96-17367   CIP

ISBN 0-393-31699-8 pbk.

W. W. Norton & Company, Inc., 500 Fifth Avenue, New York, N.Y. 10110
http://www.wwnorton.com

W. W. Norton & Company Ltd., 10 Coptic Street, London WC1A 1PU

3 4 5 6 7 8 9 0

to Hanfang

CONTENTS

FOREWORD

A good translator must turn himself into the Invisible Man: it is only if he stumbles that one should notice his existence. It would therefore appear unwise to attract the reader's attention to myself at this early stage; yet the *Analects* of Confucius has already been translated so many times that it seems necessary to explain here the nature and purpose of this new translation.

Although this work is, in a sense, the fruit of a lifetime devoted to Chinese studies, I have signed it with my literary pen name rather than with the original name under which I have taught, pursued research, and published in the field of sinology for the last thirty years. What I meant to suggest by this choice is that this is primarily a *writer's* translation; it is addressed not merely to fellow scholars, but first and foremost to nonspecialists—readers who simply wish to enlarge their cultural horizon but have no direct access to the original text.

Among the English translations of the *Analects* that are most often referred to, some are written with elegance but marred by inaccuracies; others are accurate but less felicitous in their expression. My hope is to reconcile learning with literature. This ambition may sound arrogant or presumptuous, but in fact I claim nothing more than the unfair benefit of being a latecomer. To borrow a medieval image from Bernard de Chartres, latecomers are dwarfs atop the shoulders of giants—however tiny they may be, from their vantage point they can see a little further than their mighty predecessors, and this privilege alone should fully justify their boldness.

* * *

For many of my views on Confucius, I am indebted to the teachings of Professor Lo Meng-tze, who guided me into Chinese culture thirty years ago. In his vast learning as well as in the courage and nobility of his character, Professor Lo truly displayed the virtues of a Confucian scholar. With all his friends and students, I cherish his memory.

As I was writing my first draft, Dr. Richard Rigby took the pains to read my translation chapter by chapter, patiently checking it against the original text. He raised questions and objections, he made corrections and suggestions. I am deeply grateful for his invaluable help and brotherly kindness.

Mr. Steven Forman, from Norton, was my very first reader; his perceptive comments, critical reactions, queries, and constant encouragements sustained me through the long course of this work. His support was much needed at times, and deeply appreciated. I must also give very special thanks to Mr. Robert Hemenway, for his sensitive and careful copyediting.

In acknowledgments like this, it is customary in the end to claim full responsibility for one's own views and shortcomings. I am very much tempted to break this traditional rule and to transfer all conceivable responsibilities to the account of Professor Frederick W. Mote: it was he who first suggested that I attempt this entreprise; and then, when my work was completed, he kindly undertook an attentive critical reading of my final manuscript. His scholarly endorsement has priceless value for me.

NOTE

For the transcription of Chinese names, the system adopted here is the Pinyin—less elegant (and less convenient for those who do not speak Chinese) than the Wade-Giles. This choice was dictated by the fact that the use of Pinyin is now prevalent and will probably become universal. (A table of conversion from Pinyin to Wade-Giles is provided at the end of this book.)

Regarding Chinese personal names, traditionally, Chinese were called by different names: a personal name which could be used only by parents and superiors, courtesy names for general use, fancy names, titles, etc. To avoid confusion here, as a rule every individual is referred to under only one name— even though, at times, this may grossly infringe Chinese conventions. To assess the exact identity of every character, as well as to find out his various names, readers should simply refer to the Index and to the Notes.

Regarding the Bibliography: full references are provided wherever individual works are being mentioned. The modern translations of the *Analects* which I have consulted and referred to more frequently are:

Qian Mu, *Lunyu Xin Jie*, 2 vols. (Hong Kong: Xinya Yanjiu-suo, 1963).

Yang Bojun, *Lunyu Yizhu* (Peking: Zhonghua Shuju, 1958).

Arthur Waley, *The Analects of Confucius* (London: George Allen & Unwin, 1938).

D. C. Lau, *Confucius: The Analects* (Harmondsworth: Penguin,

1979.)

Regarding explanations and comments to this translation: these are provided in the Notes (second part of this book). There are no call-outs for notes in the text of the translation; readers should check the second part directly, where all the notes are arranged under numbered headings corresponding to the chapters and paragraphs of the translation.

INTRODUCTION

Lu Xun (who is rightly considered as the greatest writer of modern China; he died in 1936, and—by the way—strongly disliked Confucius for reasons that will be briefly noted in a moment) observed that whenever a truly original genius appears in this world, people immediately endeavor to get rid of him. To this end, they have two methods. The first one is *suppression:* they isolate him, they starve him, they surround him with silence, they bury him alive. If this does not work, they adopt the second method (which is much more radical and dreadful): *exaltation*—they put him on a pedestal and they turn him into a god. (The irony, of course, is that Lu Xun himself was subjected to both treatments: when he was alive, the Communist commissars bullied him; once he was dead, they worshipped him as their holiest cultural icon—but this is another story.)

For more than two thousand years, Chinese emperors have set and promoted the official cult of Confucius. It became a sort of state religion. Now the emperors have gone (or have they?), but the cult seems very much alive still: as recently as October 1994, the Communist authorities in Peking sponsored a huge symposium to celebrate the 2545th anniversary of Confucius's birth. The main guest speaker was the former prime minister of Singapore, Lee Kuan-yew. He was invited apparently because his hosts wished to learn from him the magic recipe (supposedly found in Confucius) for marrying authoritarian politics with capitalist prosperity.

Karl Marx once warned overenthusiastic followers that he was not a Marxist. With better reason, one should say that Confucius was certainly not a Confucianist. Imperial Confucianism only extolled those statements from the Master that prescribed submission to the established authorities, whereas more essential notions were conveniently ignored—such as the precepts of social justice, political dissent, and the moral duty for intellectuals to criticize the ruler (even at the risk of their lives) when he was abusing his power, or when he oppressed the people.

As a result of these ideological manipulations, in modern times many enlightened and progressive-minded Chinese came spontaneously to associate the very name of Confucius with feudal tyranny; his doctrines became synonymous with obscurantism and oppression. All the great revolutionary movements in twentieth-century China were staunchly anti-Confucian—and it is easy enough to sympathize with them. Actually—if I may invoke here a personal experience—I still remember the dismay expressed by various Chinese friends on learning that I was translating the *Analects* of Confucius: they wondered how I could suddenly sink into that sort of intellectual and political regression.

I certainly feel no need to justify the orientation taken by my work. Yet such a justification would be all too easy to provide—for an obvious reason: no book in the entire history of the world has exerted, over a longer period of time, a greater influence on a larger number of people than this slim little volume. With its affirmation of humanist ethics and of the universal brotherhood of man, it inspired all the nations of Eastern Asia and became the spiritual cornerstone of the most populous and oldest living civilization on earth. If we do not read this book, if we do not appreciate how it was understood through the ages (and also how it was misunderstood)—how it was used (and how it was misused)—in one word, if we ignore this book, we are missing the single most important key that can give us access to the Chinese world. And whoever remains ignorant of this civilization, in the end can only reach a limited understanding of the human experience.

This consideration alone would more than justify our interest in Confucius, even if he should have been every bit as distasteful a character as so many leading Chinese intellectuals came to portray him earlier in this century. Whether he was such is not for me to say. Confucius can speak for himself—and the marvelous fact is precisely that, across twenty-five centuries, it seems at times that he is directly addressing the very problems of our age and of our society.

But this *modernity* of Confucius is an aspect which, paradoxically, non-Chinese readers may perhaps be in a better position to appreciate. The only advantage that can be derived from our condition of ignorant foreigners is precisely the possibility to look with a kind of unbiased innocence at this book—as if it were all fresh and new. Such innocence is denied to native readers. For them, the *Analects* is *the* classic *par excellence*. And before proceeding further, we should first briefly consider what is implied by the notion of a "classic."

The nature of a classic

A classic is essentially a text that is open-ended—in the sense that it lends itself constantly to new developments, new commentaries, different interpretations. With the passing of time, these commentaries, interpretations, and glosses form a series of layers, deposits, accretions, alluvions, that accumulate, accrue, superpose on one another, like the sands and sediments of a silting-up river. A classic allows for countless uses and misuses, understandings and misunderstandings; it is a text that keeps growing—it can be deformed, it can be enriched—and yet it retains its core identity, even if its original shape cannot be fully retrieved anymore. In an interview, Jorge Luis Borges once said: "Readers create anew the books they read. Shakespeare is more rich today than when he wrote. Cervantes too. Cervantes was enriched by Unamuno; Shakespeare was enriched by Coleridge, by Bradley. That's how a writer grows. After his death, he continues to develop in the minds of his readers. And the Bible, for instance, today is richer than when its various parts were first written. A book benefits from the passing of time. Everything can be of benefit to it. Even misunderstandings may help an author. Everything helps—even readers' ignorance or carelessness. After you have read a book, you may retain an inaccurate impression of it—but this means that it is being amended by your memory. That happens often to me. Caramba! I don't know whether I dare to confess this—but whenever I quote Shakespeare, I realize that I have improved on him!"

In a sense (if I may use such a trivial image) the way in which every statement in a classic can gather the comments of posterity may be compared to a hook, or a peg on the wall of a cloakroom. Successive users of the cloakroom come one after the other and hang on the peg hats, coats, umbrellas, bags and what not; the load swells up, heavy, colorful, diversified, and eventually the hook disappears entirely under it. For the native reader the classic is intricate and crowded, it is a place filled with people, and voices, and things and memories—vibrating with echoes. For the foreign reader, on the contrary, the classic often presents the forlorn aspect of the cloakroom after hours—an empty room with mere rows of bare hooks on a blank wall, and this extreme austerity, this stark and disconcerting simplicity account in part for the paradoxical impression of *modernity* which he is more likely to experience.

The Analects and the Gospels

The *Analects* is the only place where we can actually encounter the real, living Confucius. In this sense, the *Analects* is to Confucius what the Gospels are to Jesus. The text, which consists of a discontinuous series of brief statements, short dialogues and anecdotes, was compiled by two successive generations of disciples (disciples and disciples of disciples), over some seventy-five years after Confucius's death—which means that the compilation was probably completed a little before, or around, 400 B.C. The text is a patchwork: fragments from different hands have been stitched together, with uneven skill—there are some repetitions, interpolations, and contradictions; there are some puzzles and countless loopholes; but on the whole, there are very few stylistic anachronisms: the language and syntax of most of the fragments is coherent and pertains to the same period.[1]

On one essential point the comparison with the Gospels proves particularly enlightening. Textual problems have led some modern scholars to question the credibility of the Gospels, and even to doubt the historical existence of Christ. These studies have provoked lately an intriguing reaction from an unlikely source: Julien Gracq—an old and prestigious novelist, who was close to the Surrealist movement—made a comment which is all the more arresting for coming from an

agnostic. In a recent volume of essays,[2] Gracq first acknowledged the impressive learning of one of these scholars (whose
lectures he had attended in his youth), as well as the devastating logic of his reasoning; but he confessed that, in the end,
he still found himself left with one fundamental objection: for
all his formidable erudition, the scholar in question had simply
no *ear*—he could not *hear* what should be so obvious to any
sensitive reader—that, underlying the text of the Gospels,
there is a masterly and powerful unity of style, which derives
from one unique and inimitable voice; there is the presence of
one singular and exceptional personality whose expression is
so original, so bold that one could positively call it *impudent.*
Now, if you deny the existence of Jesus, you must transfer
all these attributes to some obscure, anonymous writer, who
should have had the improbable genius of inventing such a
character—or, even more implausibly, you must transfer this
prodigious capacity for invention to an entire committee of
writers. And Gracq concluded: in the end, if modern scholars,
progressive-minded clerics, and the docile public all surrender
to this critical erosion of the Scriptures, the last group of
defenders who will obstinately maintain that there *is* a living
Jesus at the central core of the Gospels will be made of artists
and creative writers, for whom the psychological evidence of
style carries much more weight than mere philological argu-
ments.

Who was Confucius?

Having noted why and how a novelist could perceive an
essential aspect of the Gospels which a scholar had failed to
grasp, it is time now to return to Confucius: there is naturally
no need to defend his historical existence—it was never put

into question—but any reader of the *Analects* ought certainly to develop the sort of sensitivity which Gracq displayed in his reading of the Gospels, and become similarly attuned to Confucius's unique voice. The strong and complex individuality of the Master is the very backbone of the book, and defines its unity. Elias Canetti (to whom I shall return later on) summed it up neatly: "The *Analects* of Confucius are the oldest complete intellectual and spiritual portrait of a man. It strikes one as a modern book."

Traditional historiography tells us that Confucius was born in 551 and died in 479 B.C. (These dates may not be accurate, but modern scholarship has nothing better to offer.)

Over the centuries, the official Confucian cult has created a conventional image of the Master, and as a result, many people have tended to imagine him as a solemn old preacher, always proper, a bit pompous, slightly boring—one of these men who "push moderation too far." In refreshing contrast with these common stereotypes, the *Analects* reveals a living Confucius that constantly surprises. In one passage, for instance, the Master provides an intriguing self-portrait: the governor of a certain town had asked one of the disciples what sort of man Confucius was, and the disciple did not know how to reply, which provoked Confucius's reaction: "Why did you not simply tell him that Confucius is a man driven by so much passion that, in his enthusiasm, he often forgets to eat and remains unaware of the onset of old age?"

That Confucius should have chosen *enthusiasm* as the main defining aspect of his character is revealing, and is further confirmed by other episodes and statements in the *Analects*. For example, after Confucius listened to a rare piece of ancient music, we are told, the emotion took him by surprise; "for three months, he forgot the taste of meat." Elsewhere again, he stated that love and ecstasy were superior forms of knowl-

edge. On various occasions he could also upset and shock his
entourage. When his beloved disciple Yan Hui died prema-
turely, Confucius was devastated; his grief was wild, he cried
with a violence that stunned people around him; they objected
that such an excessive reaction did not befit a sage—a criticism which Confucius rejected indignantly.

In contrast with the idealized image of the traditional
scholar, frail and delicate, living among books, the *Analects*
shows that Confucius was adept at outdoor activities: he was
an accomplished sportsman, he was expert at handling horses,
he practised archery, he was fond of hunting and fishing. He
was a bold and tireless traveler in a time when travel was a
difficult and hazardous adventure; he was constantly moving
from country to country (pre-imperial China was a mosaic of
autonomous states, speaking different dialects but sharing a
common culture—a situation somewhat comparable with that
of modern Europe). At times, he was in great physical danger,
and narrowly escaped ambushes set by his political enemies.
Once, in despair at his lack of success in trying to convert the
civilized world to his ways, he contemplated going abroad and
settling among the barbarians. On another occasion, he toyed
with the idea of sailing away on a seagoing raft, such as were
used in his time for ocean voyages (this daring plan was to
puzzle to no end the less adventurous scholars of later ages).

Confucius was a man of action—audacious and heroic—but
ultimately he was also a tragic figure. This has perhaps not
been sufficiently perceived.

The fundamental misconception that developed regarding
Confucius is summed up by the label under which imperial
China undertook to worship him—and at the same time, to
neutralize the subversive potential originally contained in his
political message. For two thousand years, Confucius was can-
onized as China's First and Supreme *Teacher* (his birthday—

September 28—is still celebrated as Teachers Day in China). This is a cruel irony. Of course, Confucius devoted much attention to education but he never considered teaching as his first and real calling. His true vocation was politics. He had a mystical faith in his political mission.

Confucius lived in a period of historical transition, in an age of acute cultural crisis. In one fundamental respect, there was a certain similarity between his time and ours: *he was witnessing the collapse of civilization*—he saw his world sinking into violence and barbarity. Five hundred years before him, a universal feudal order had been established, unifying the entire civilized world: this was the achievement of one of China's greatest cultural heroes, the Duke of Zhou. But now the Zhou tradition was no longer operative, the Zhou world was falling apart. Confucius believed that Heaven had chosen him to become the spiritual heir to the Duke of Zhou, and that he should revive his grand design, restore the world order on a new ethical basis, and salvage the entire civilization.

The *Analects* is suffused with the unshakable belief which Confucius had in his Heavenly mission. He constantly prepared for it, and actually the recruitment and training of his disciples was part of his political plan. He spent virtually his entire life wandering from state to state, in the hope of finding an enlightened ruler who would at last give him a chance, and employ him and his team—who would entrust him with a territory, however small, where he might establish a model government. All his efforts were in vain. The problem was not that he was politically ineffectual or impractical—on the contrary. The elite of his disciples had superior competences and talents, and they formed around him a sort of shadow cabinet: there was a specialist in foreign affairs and diplomacy, there were experts in finances, administration, and defense. With such a team, Confucius presented a formidable challenge to the established authorities: dukes and princes felt incapable of performing up to his standards, and their respective ministers knew that, should Confucius and his disciples ever get a foothold at court, they themselves would quickly be without employment. Wherever he went, Confucius was usually received with much respect and formal courtesy at first; in practice, however, not only did he find no political opening, but cabals eventually forced him to leave. Sometimes, even, local hostility swiftly developed and, quite literally, he had to run for his life. Early in his career, Confucius had once, briefly, been in office at a fairly low level; after that, never again in his life was he to occupy any official position.

From this point of view, one may truly say that Confucius's career was a total and colossal failure. An admiring posterity of disciples were reluctant to contemplate this stark reality: the humiliating failure of a spiritual leader is always a most disturbing paradox which the ordinary faithful cannot easily come to terms with. (Consider again the case of Jesus: it took three hundred years before Christians became able to confront the *image* of the cross.[3])

Thus, the tragic reality of Confucius as failed politician was replaced by the glorious myth of Confucius the Supreme Teacher.

The politics of Confucius

Politics—as I have just indicated—was Confucius's first and foremost concern; but, more generally, this is also true of ancient Chinese philosophy. On the whole (with the only *sublime* exception of the Daoist Zhuang Zi), early Chinese thought essentially revolved around two questions: the harmony of the universe and the harmony of society—in other words, cosmology and politics.

The eremitic life may be tempting for a sage; but since we are not birds nor beasts, we cannot escape among them. We must associate with our fellowmen. And when the world loses the Way, the sage has a moral duty to reform society and to set it back on track.

Politics is an extension of ethics:[4] "Government is synonymous with righteousness. If the king is righteous, how could anyone dare to be crooked?" The government is of men, not of laws (to this very day, this remains one of the most dangerous flaws in the Chinese political tradition). Confucius had a deep distrust of laws: laws invite people to become tricky, and bring out the worst in them. The true cohesion of a society is secured not through legal rules but through ritual observances. The central importance of *rites* in the Confucian order may at first appear disconcerting to some Western readers (conjuring up in their minds quaint images of smiling Oriental gentlemen, bowing endlessly to each other), but the oddity is merely semantic; one needs only to substitute for the word "rites" concepts such as *"moeurs,"* "civilized usages," "moral conventions," or even "common decency," and one immediately realizes that the Confucian values are remarkably close to the principles of political philosophy which the Western world inherited from the Enlightenment. Montesquieu in particular (who, paradoxically, did not share in the Chinese euphoria of his time, as he detected a ruthless despotism at work in the political practice of eighteenth-century China) developed notions which unwittingly recouped Confucius's views that a government of rites is to be preferred to a government of laws; Montesquieu considered that an increase in law-making activity was not a sign of civilization—it indicated on the contrary a breakdown of social morality, and his famous statement *"Quand un peuple a de bonnes mœurs, les lois deviennent simples"* could have been lifted straight from the *Analects.*

According to Confucius, a king leads by his moral power. If he cannot set a moral example—if he cannot maintain and promote rituals and music (the two hallmarks of civilization), he forfeits the loyalty of his ministers and the trust of the people. The ultimate asset of the state is the trust of the people in their rulers: if that trust is lost, the country is doomed.

Confucius often said that, if only a ruler could employ him, in one year he would achieve a lot, and in three years he would succeed. One day, a disciple asked him: "If a king were to entrust you with a territory which you could govern according to your ideas, what would you do first?" Confucius replied: "My first task would certainly be *to rectify the names."* On hearing this, the disciple was puzzled: "Rectify the names? And that would be your first priority? Is this a joke?" (Chesterton or Orwell, however, would have immediately understood and approved the idea.) Confucius had to explain: "If the names are not correct, if they do not match realities, language has no object. If language is without an object, action becomes impossible—and therefore, all human affairs disintegrate and their management becomes pointless and impossible. Hence, the very first task of a true statesman is to rectify the names."

And this is, in fact, what Confucius himself endeavored to do. One can read the *Analects* as an attempt to redefine the true sense of a series of key concepts. Under the guise of restoring their full meaning, Confucius actually injected a new content into the old "names." Here I shall give only one example, but it is of momentous importance: the notion of "gentleman" (*junzi,* Confucius's ideal man). Originally it meant an aristocrat, a member of the *social* elite: one did not become a gentleman, one could only be *born* a gentleman. For Confucius, on the contrary, the "gentleman" is a member of the *moral* elite. It is an ethical quality, achieved by the practice of virtue, and secured through education. Every man should strive for it, even though few may reach it. An aristocrat who is immoral and uneducated (the two notions of morality and learning are synonymous) is not a gentleman, whereas any commoner can attain the status of gentleman if he proves morally qualified. As only gentlemen are fit to rule, political authority should be devolved purely on the criteria of moral achievement and intellectual competence. Therefore, in a proper state of affairs, neither birth nor money should secure power. Political authority should pertain exclusively to those who can demonstrate moral and intellectual qualifications.

This view was to have revolutionary consequences: it was the single most devastating ideological blow that furthered the destruction of the feudal system and sapped the power of the hereditary aristocracy, and it led eventually to the establishment of the bureaucratic empire—the government of the scholars. For more than two thousand years, the empire was to be ruled by the intellectual elite; to gain access to political power, one had to compete successfully in the civil service examinations, which were open to all. Until modern times, this was certainly the most open, flexible, fair, and sophisticated system of government known in history (it is the very system which was to impress and inspire the European *philosophes* of the eighteenth century).

Confucius on education

It is often remarked that the most successful and dynamic societies of East and South-East Asia (Japan, Korea, Taiwan,

Hong Kong, and Singapore) share a common Confucian culture. Should one therefore conclude that the *Analects* might actually yield a secret formula that would make it possible elsewhere to inject energy into flagging economies, and to mobilize and motivate a slovenly citizenry?

The prosperity of a modern state is a complex phenomenon that can hardly be ascribed to one single factor. Yet there is indeed one common feature that characterizes the various "Confucian" societies—but it should be observed that this same feature can also be found in other social or ethnic groups (for instance, certain Jewish communities of the Western world) which are equally creative and prosperous, and yet do not present any connection with the Confucian tradition; and it is the extraordinary importance which these societies all attach to *education*. Any government, any community, or any family which would be willing to invest in education as considerable a proportion of its energy and resources should be bound to reap cultural, social, and economic benefits comparable to those which are currently achieved by the thriving "Confucian" states of Asia, or by some dynamic and wealthy migrant minorities of the Western world.

In affirming that the government and administration of the state should be exclusively entrusted to a moral and intellectual elite of "gentlemen," Confucius established an enduring and decisive link between education and political power: only the former could provide access to the latter. In modern times, even after the abrogation of the civil service examination system and the fall of the empire, although education ceased to be the key to political authority,—which in this new situation was more likely to come out of the barrel of a gun—the prestige traditionally attached to culture continued to survive in the mentality of the Confucian societies: the educated man, however poor and powerless, still commanded more respect than the wealthy or the powerful.

Confucian education was open to all indifferently—rich and poor, noble and plebeian. Its purpose was primarily *moral:* intellectual achievement was only a means towards ethical self-cultivation. There was an optimistic belief in the all-pervasive power of education: it was assumed that errant behavior came from a faulty understanding, a lack of knowledge: if only the delinquent could be taught, and be made to perceive the mistaken nature of his actions, he would naturally amend his ways. (The Maoist concept of "re-education" that was to generate such dreadful excesses at the time of the "Cultural Revolution" was in fact one of the many unconscious resurgences of the Confucian mentality, which paradoxically permeated the psychological substructure of Maoism.)

Most importantly, Confucian education was humanistic and universalist. As the Master said: "A gentleman is not a pot" (or also: "A gentleman is not a tool")—meaning that his capacity should not have a specific limit, nor his usefulness a narrow application. What matters is not to accumulate technical information and specialized expertise, but to develop one's humanity. Education is not about *having,* it is about *being.*

Confucius once rebuffed quite rudely a disciple who had asked him about agronomy: "Better ask any old peasant!" For this reason, it is often alleged now that Confucianism inhibited the development of science and technology in China. But there are no real grounds for such an accusation. Simply, in these matters Confucius's concerns centered on education and culture—not on training and technique, which are separate issues altogether—and it is difficult to see how one could address these topics any differently, whether in Confucius's time or in ours. (C. P. Snow's famous notion of the "Two Cultures" rested on a basic fallacy: it ignored that, like humanity itself, culture can only be one, by its very definition. I have no doubt that a scientist can be—and probably should be—better cultivated than a philosopher, a latinist, or a historian, but if he is, it is because he reads philosophy, Latin, and history in his leisure time.)

The silences of Confucius

In the short essay he wrote on Confucius, Elias Canetti (whom I quoted earlier) made a point that had escaped most scholars.[5] He observed that the *Analects* is a book which is important not only for what it says, but also for what it does *not* say. This remark is illuminating. Indeed, the *Analects* makes a most significant use of the unsaid—which is also a characteristic resource of the Chinese mind; it was eventually to find some of its most expressive applications in the field of aesthetics: the use of silence in music, the use of void in painting, the use of empty spaces in architecture.

Confucius distrusted eloquence; he despised glib talkers, he hated clever word games. For him, it would seem that an agile tongue must reflect a shallow mind; as reflection runs deeper, silence develops. Confucius observed that his favorite disciple used to say so little that, at times, one could have wondered if he was not an idiot. To another disciple who had asked him about the supreme virtue of humanity, Confucius replied characteristically: "He who possesses the supreme virtue of humanity is reluctant to speak."

The essential is beyond words: all that can be said is superfluous. Therefore a disciple remarked: "We can hear and gather our Master's teachings in matters of knowledge and culture, but it is impossible to make him speak on the ultimate nature of things, or on the will of Heaven." This silence reflected no indifference or scepticism regarding the will of Heaven—we know from many passages in the *Analects* that Confucius regarded it as *the* supreme guide of his life; but Confucius would have subscribed to Wittgenstein's famous conclusion: "Whereof one cannot speak, thereof one must be silent." He did not deny the reality of what is beyond words, he merely warned against the foolishness of attempting to reach it with words. His silence was an affirmation: there *is* a realm about which one can say nothing.

Confucius's silences occurred essentially when his interlocutors tried to draw him into the question of the afterlife. This attitude has often led commentators to conclude that Confucius was an agnostic. Such a conclusion seems to me very shallow. Consider this famous passage: "Zilu asked about death. The Master said: 'You do not know life; how could you know death?'" Canetti added this comment: "I know of no sages who took death as seriously as Confucius." Refusal to answer is not a way of evading the issue, but on the contrary, it is its most forceful affirmation, for questions about death, in fact, always "refer to a time *after* death. Any answer leaps past death, conjuring away both death and its incomprehensibility. If there is something *afterwards* as there was something *before*, then death loses some of its weight. Confucius refuses to play along with this most unworthy legerdemain."

Like the empty space in a painting—which concentrates and radiates all the inner energy of the painting—Confucius's silence is not a withdrawal or an escape; it leads to a deeper and closer engagement into life and reality. Near the end of his career, Confucius said one day to his disciples: "I wish to speak no more." The disciples were perplexed: "But, Master, if you do not speak, how would little ones like us still be able to hand down any teachings?" Confucius replied: "Does

Heaven speak? Yet the four seasons follow their course and the hundred creatures continue to be born. Does Heaven speak?"

I have certainly spoken too much.

1. On these problems of chronology and textual analysis, see the forthcoming work of E. Bruce Brooks (to be published by Columbia University Press).

2. Julien Gracq, *Les carnets du grand chemin* (Paris: José Corti, 1992), 190–91.

3. The earliest images of the cross discovered by archaeology were *anti-Christian* graffiti, whereas the art of the Catacombs only used abstract symbols to represent Christ. The cross was a hideous instrument of torture, a reminder of abject humiliation and death; it is only in the time of Constantine that it began to be displayed as a triumphant symbol of victory over evil; and yet it still took nearly another thousand years before medieval artists dared to represent *the dead Christ hanging on it.*

4. Most of the notions which are raised in this Introduction are further analyzed in my Notes. As many readers do not read notes (they do not know what they are missing!), at the risk of being repetitive, I am first outlining here some of the major themes that are more fully developed in the second part of this book.

5. Elias Canetti, *The Conscience of Words* (New York: Seabury Press, 1979), 171–75.

The
Analects
of
Confucius

Chapter

1

1.1.　The Master said: "To learn something and then to put it into practice at the right time: is this not a joy? To have friends coming from afar: is this not a delight? Not to be upset when one's merits are ignored: is this not the mark of a gentleman?" *

1.2.　Master You said: "A man who respects his parents and his elders would hardly be inclined to defy his superiors. A man who is not inclined to defy his superiors will never foment a rebellion. A gentleman works at the root. Once the root is secured, the Way unfolds. To respect parents and elders is the root of humanity."

1.3.　The Master said: "Clever talk and affected manners are seldom signs of goodness."

1.4.　Master Zeng said: "I examine myself three times a day. When dealing on behalf of others, have I been trustworthy?

* For explanations and comments, readers should refer to the second part of this book, where all the notes are collected under numbered headings corresponding to the chapters and paragraphs of the translation. No further callouts for notes appear in the text of the translation.

In intercourse with my friends, have I been faithful? Have I practiced what I was taught?"

1.5. The Master said: "To govern a state of middle size, one must dispatch business with dignity and good faith; be thrifty and love all men; mobilize the people only at the right times."

1.6. The Master said: "At home, a young man must respect his parents; abroad, he must respect his elders. He should talk little, but with good faith; love all people, but associate with the virtuous. Having done this, if he still has energy to spare, let him study literature."

1.7. Zixia said: "A man who values virtue more than good looks, who devotes all his energy to serving his father and mother, who is willing to give his life for his sovereign, who in intercourse with friends is true to his word—even though some may call him uneducated, I still maintain he is an educated man."

1.8. The Master said: "A gentleman who lacks gravity has no authority and his learning will remain shallow. A gentleman puts loyalty and faithfulness foremost; he does not befriend his moral inferiors. When he commits a fault, he is not afraid to amend his ways."

1.9. Master Zeng said: "When the dead are honored and the memory of remote ancestors is kept alive, a people's virtue is at its fullest."

1.10. Ziqin asked Zigong: "When the Master arrives in another country, he always becomes informed about its politics. Does he ask for such information, or is it given him?" Zigong replied: "The Master obtains it by being cordial, kind, courteous, temperate, and deferential. The Master has a way of enquiring which is quite different from other people's, is it not?"

1.11. The Master said: "When the father is alive, watch the son's aspirations. When the father is dead, watch the son's actions. If three years later, the son has not veered from the father's way, he may be called a dutiful son indeed."

1.12. Master You said: "When practicing the ritual, what matters most is harmony. This is what made the beauty of the way of the ancient kings; it inspired their every move, great or small. Yet they knew where to stop: harmony cannot be sought for its own sake, it must always be subordinated to the ritual; otherwise it would not do."

1.13. Master You said: "If your promises conform to what is right, you will be able to keep your word. If your manners conform to the ritual, you will be able to keep shame and disgrace at bay. The best support is provided by one's own kinsmen."

1.14. The Master said: "A gentleman eats without stuffing his belly; chooses a dwelling without demanding comfort; is diligent in his office and prudent in his speech; seeks the company of the virtuous in order to straighten his own ways. Of such a man, one may truly say that he is fond of learning."

1.15. Zigong said: " 'Poor without servility; rich without arrogance.' How is that?" The Master said: "Not bad, but better still: 'Poor, yet cheerful; rich, yet considerate.' " Zigong said: "In the *Poems*, it is said: 'Like carving horn, like sculpting ivory, like cutting jade, like polishing stone.' Is this not the same idea?" The Master said: "Ah, one can really begin to discuss the *Poems* with you! I tell you one thing, and you can figure out the rest."

1.16. The Master said: "Don't worry if people don't recognize your merits; worry that you may not recognize theirs."

Chapter

2

2.1 The Master said: "He who rules by virtue is like the polestar, which remains unmoving in its mansion while all the other stars revolve respectfully around it."

2.2. The Master said: "The three hundred *Poems* are summed up in one single phrase: 'Think no evil.'"

2.3. The Master said: "Lead them by political maneuvers, restrain them with punishments: the people will become cunning and shameless. Lead them by virtue, restrain them with ritual: they will develop a sense of shame and a sense of participation."

2.4. The Master said: "At fifteen, I set my mind upon learning. At thirty, I took my stand. At forty, I had no doubts. At fifty, I knew the will of Heaven. At sixty, my ear was attuned. At seventy, I follow all the desires of my heart without breaking any rule."

2.5. Lord Meng Yi asked about filial piety. The Master said: "Never disobey."

As Fan Chi was driving him in his chariot, the Master told him: "Meng Yi asked me about filial piety and I replied: 'Never disobey.'" Fan Chi said: "What does that mean?" The Master said: "When your parents are alive, serve them according to the ritual. When they die, bury them according to the ritual, make sacrifices to them according to the ritual."

2.6.   Lord Meng Wu asked about filial piety. The Master said: "The only time a dutiful son ever makes his parents worry is when he is sick."

2.7.   Ziyou asked about filial piety. The Master said: "Nowadays people think they are dutiful sons when they feed their parents. Yet they also feed their dogs and horses. Unless there is respect, where is the difference?"

2.8.   Zixia asked about filial piety. The Master said: "It is the attitude that matters. If young people merely offer their services when there is work to do, or let their elders drink and eat when there is wine and food, how could this ever pass as filial piety?"

2.9.   The Master said: "I can talk all day to Yan Hui—he never raises any objection, he looks stupid. Yet, observe him when he is on his own: his actions fully reflect what he learned. Oh no, Hui is not stupid!"

2.10.   The Master said: "Find out why a man acts, observe how he acts, and examine where he finds his peace. Is there anything he could still hide?"

2.11.   The Master said: "He who by revising the old knows the new, is fit to be a teacher."

2.12.   The Master said: "A gentleman is not a pot."

2.13.   Zigong asked about the true gentleman. The Master said: "He preaches only what he practices."

2.14.   The Master said: "The gentleman considers the whole rather than the parts. The small man considers the parts rather than the whole."

2.15.   The Master said: "To study without thinking is futile. To think without studying is dangerous."

2.16.   The Master said: "To attack a question from the wrong end—this is harmful indeed."

2.17.   The Master said: "Zilu, I am going to teach you what knowledge is. To take what you know for what you know, and what you do not know for what you do not know, that is knowledge indeed."

2.18.   Zizhang was studying in the hope of securing an official position. The Master said: "Collect much information, put aside what is doubtful, repeat cautiously the rest; then you will seldom say something wrong. Make many observations, leave aside what is suspect, apply cautiously the rest; then you will seldom have cause for regret. With few mistakes in what you say and few regrets for what you do, your career is made."

2.19.   Duke Ai asked: "What should I do to win the hearts of the people?" Confucius replied: "Raise the straight and set them above the crooked, and you will win the hearts of the people. If you raise the crooked and set them above the straight, the people will deny you their support."

2.20.   Lord Ji Kang asked: "What should I do in order to make the people respectful, loyal, and zealous?" The Master said: "Approach them with dignity and they will be respectful. Be yourself a good son and a kind father, and they will be loyal. Raise the good and train the incompetent, and they will be zealous."

2.21.   Someone said to Confucius: "Master, why don't you join the government?" The Master said: "In the *Documents* it is said: 'Only cultivate filial piety and be kind to your brothers, and you will be contributing to the body politic.' This is also a form of political action; one need not necessarily join the government."

2.22. The Master said: "If a man cannot be trusted, I wouldn't know what to do with him. How would you pull a wagon without a yoke-bar or a chariot without a collar-bar?"

2.23. Zizhang asked: "Can we know the future ten generations hence?" The Master said: "Yin borrowed from the ritual of Xia: we can know what was dropped and what was added. Zhou borrowed from the ritual of Yin: we can know what was dropped and what was added. If Zhou has successors, we can know what they will be like, even a hundred generations hence."

2.24. The Master said: "To worship gods that are not yours, that is toadyism. Not to act when justice commands, that is cowardice."

3.1   The head of the Ji Family used eight rows of dancers in the ceremonies of his ancestral temple. Confucius commented: "If he is capable of that, what will he not be capable of?"

3.2.   The Three Families performed the poem *Yong* at the end of their ancestral sacrifices. The Master said: "This poem says:

> The feudal lords are in attendance,
> The Son of Heaven is sitting on his throne.

What application can this have in the halls of the Three Families?"

3.3.   The Master said: "If a man has no humanity, what can he have to do with ritual? If a man has no humanity, what can he have to do with music?"

3.4.   Lin Fang asked: "What is the root of ritual?" The Master said: "Big question! In ceremonies, prefer simplicity to lavishness; in funerals, prefer grief to formality."

3.5.   The Master said: "Barbarians who have rulers are inferior to the various nations of China who are without."

3.6.   The Head of the Ji Family was setting out on a royal pilgrimage to Mount Tai. The Master said to Ran Qiu: "Cannot you prevent this?" Ran Qiu replied: "I cannot." The Master said: "Alas! has it ever been said that the Spirit of Mount Tai had even less ritual knowledge than Lin Fang?"

3.7.   The Master said: "A gentleman avoids competition. Still, if he must compete let it be at archery. There, as he bows and exchanges civilities both before the contest and over drinks afterward, he remains a gentleman, even in competition."

3.8.   Zixia asked: "What do these verses mean:

> Oh, the dimples of her smile!
> Ah, the black and white of her beautiful eyes!
> It is on plain white silk that colors shine.

The Master said: "Painting starts from a plain white silk." Zixia said: "Ritual is something that comes afterward?" The Master said: "Ah, you really opened my eyes! It is only with a man like you that one can discuss the *Poems!*"

3.9.   The Master said: "Can I talk about Xia ritual? Its inheritor, the country of Qi, has not preserved sufficient evidence. Can I talk about Yin ritual? Its inheritor, the country of Song, has not preserved sufficient evidence. There are not enough records and not enough wise men; otherwise, I could draw evidence from them."

3.10.   The Master said: "At the sacrifice to the Ancestor of the Dynasty, once the first libation has been performed, I do not wish to watch the rest."

3.11.   Someone asked Confucius to explain the meaning of the sacrifice to the Ancestor of the Dynasty. The Master said: "I do not know. Whoever knew that would master the world as if he had it in the palm of his hand." And he put his finger in his hand.

3.12.   Sacrifice implies presence. One should sacrifice to the gods as if they were present. The Master said: "If I do not sacrifice with my whole heart, I might as well not sacrifice."

3.13.   Wangsun Jia asked: "What does this saying mean: 'Flatter the god of the kitchen rather than the god of the house' "? The Master said: "Nonsense. If you offend Heaven, prayer is useless."

3.14.   The Master said: "The Zhou dynasty modeled itself upon the two preceding dynasties. What a splendid civilization! I am a follower of Zhou."

3.15.   The Master visited the grand temple of the Founder of the Dynasty. He enquired about everything. Someone said: "Who said this fellow was expert on ritual? When visiting the grand temple, he had to enquire about everything." Hearing of this, the Master said: "Precisely, this is ritual."

3.16.   The Master said: "In archery, it does not matter whether one pierces the target, for archers may be of uneven strength. Such was the view of the ancients."

3.17.   Zigong wished to dispense with the sacrifice of a sheep for the New Moon Ceremony. The Master said: "You love the sheep—I love the ceremony."

3.18.   The Master said: "When a man serves his lord in complete observance of the ritual, people think he is a sycophant."

3.19.   Duke Ding asked: "How should a ruler treat his minister? How should a minister serve his ruler?" Confucius replied: "A ruler should treat his minister with courtesy, a minister should serve his ruler with loyalty."

3.20. The Master said: "The poem *The Ospreys* is gay without lasciviousness and sad without bitterness."

3.21. Duke Ai asked Zai Yu which wood should be used for the local totem. Zai Yu replied: "The men of Xia used pine; the men of Yin used cypress; the men of Zhou used *fir*, for (they said) the people should *fear*."

The Master heard of this; he said: "What is done is done, it is all past; there would be no point in arguing."

3.22. The Master said: "Guan Zhong was of mediocre calibre indeed!" Someone objected: "Wasn't Guan Zhong frugal?" He replied: "Guan Zhong had three palaces, each one fully serviced. How could he be called frugal?"—"Yet, didn't he know the ritual?"—"Only the ruler of a state can set a screen in his gate; but Guan Zhong too set a screen in his gate. Only the ruler of a state, when meeting with another ruler, can use a special stand to rest his cup, but Guan Zhong too used such a stand. If you say that Guan Zhong knew the ritual, then who does not know the ritual?"

3.23. The Master was talking about music with the music master of Lu. He said: "What we can know of music is only this: first, there is an opening passage with all instruments in unison; from there it flows harmoniously, clearly, and continuously; and then it ends."

3.24. The officer in charge of the border at Yi requested an interview with Confucius. He said: "Whenever a gentleman comes to these parts, I always ask to see him." The disciples arranged an interview. When it was over, the officer said to them: "Gentlemen, do not worry about his dismissal. The world has been without the Way for a long while. Heaven is going to use your master to ring the tocsin."

3.25. Of the Hymn of Peaceful Coronation, the Master said that it was utterly beautiful and utterly good. Of the Hymn of Military Conquest, he said that it was utterly beautiful, but not utterly good.

3.26. The Master said: "Authority without generosity, ceremony without reverence, mourning without grief—these, I cannot bear to contemplate."

Chapter

4

4.1. The Master said: "It is beautiful to live amidst humanity. To choose a dwelling place destitute of humanity is hardly wise."

4.2. The Master said: "A man without humanity cannot long bear adversity and cannot long know joy. A good man rests in his humanity, a wise man profits from his humanity."

4.3. The Master said: "Only a good man can love people and can hate people."

4.4. The Master said: "Seeking to achieve humanity leaves no room for evil."

4.5. The Master said: "Riches and rank are what every man craves; yet if the only way to obtain them goes against his principles, he should desist from such a pursuit. Poverty and obscurity are what every man hates; yet if the only escape from them goes against his principles, he should accept his lot. If a gentleman forsakes humanity, how can he make a name for himself? Never for a moment does a gentleman part from humanity; he clings to it through trials, he clings to it through tribulations."

4.6. The Master said: "I have never seen a man who truly loved goodness and hated evil. Whoever truly loves goodness would put nothing above it; whoever truly hates evil would practice goodness in such a way that no evil could enter him. Has anyone ever devoted all his strength to goodness just for one day? No one ever has, and yet it is not for want of strength—there may be people who do not have even the small amount of strength it takes, but I have never seen any."

4.7.   The Master said: "Your faults define you. From your very faults one can know your quality."

4.8.   The Master said: "In the morning hear the Way; in the evening die content."

4.9.   The Master said: "A scholar sets his heart on the Way; if he is ashamed of his shabby clothes and coarse food, he is not worth listening to."

4.10.   The Master said: "In the affairs of the world, a gentleman has no parti pris: he takes the side of justice."

4.11.   The Master said: "A gentleman seeks virtue; a small man seeks land. A gentleman seeks justice; a small man seeks favors."

4.12.   The Master said: "He who acts out of self-interest arouses much resentment."

4.13.   The Master said: "If one can govern the country by observing ritual and showing deference, there is no more to be said. If one cannot govern the country by observing ritual and showing deference, what's the use of ritual?"

4.14.   The Master said: "Do not worry if you are without a position; worry lest you do not deserve a position. Do not worry if you are not famous; worry lest you do not deserve to be famous."

4.15. The Master said: "Shen, my doctrine has one single thread running through it." Master Zeng Shen replied: "Indeed."

The Master left. The other disciples asked: "What did he mean?" Master Zeng said: "The doctrine of the Master is: Loyalty and reciprocity, and that's all."

4.16. The Master said: "A gentleman considers what is just; a small man considers what is expedient."

4.17. The Master said: "When you see a worthy man, seek to emulate him. When you see an unworthy man, examine yourself."

4.18. The Master said: "When you serve your parents, you may gently remonstrate with them. If you see that they do not take your advice, be all the more respectful and do not contradict them. Let not your efforts turn to bitterness."

4.19. The Master said: "While your parents are alive, do not travel afar. If you have to travel, you must leave an address."

4.20. The Master said: "If three years after his father's death, the son does not alter his father's ways, he is a good son indeed."

4.21. The Master said: "Always keep in mind the age of your parents. Let this thought be both your joy and your worry."

4.22. The Master said: "The ancients were reluctant to speak, fearing disgrace should their deeds not match their words."

4.23. The Master said: "Self-control seldom leads astray."

4.24. The Master said: "A gentleman should be slow to speak and prompt to act."

4.25. The Master said: "Virtue is not solitary; it always has neighbors."

4.26. Ziyou said: "In the service of one's lord, pettiness brings disgrace; in friendly intercourse, pettiness brings estrangement."

5.1. The Master said of Gongye Chang: "He would make a good husband. Although he has been in jail, he was innocent." He gave him his daughter in marriage.

5.2. The Master said of Nan Rong: "In a country where the Way prevails, he will not be overlooked. In a country without the Way, he will still save his skin." He gave him his niece in marriage.

5.3. The Master said of Zijian: "What a true gentleman! If there were in truth no gentlemen in Lu, where could he have acquired his qualities?"

5.4. Zigong asked: "What do you think of me?" The Master said: "You are a pot."—"What sort of pot?"—"A precious ritual vase."

5.5. Someone said: "Ran Yong is good but not eloquent." The Master said: "What is the use of eloquence? An agile tongue creates many enemies. Whether Ran Yong is good, I do not know; but he certainly has no need for eloquence."

5.6. The Master recommended Qidiao Kai for an official position, but the other replied: "I am not up to the task yet." The Master was delighted.

5.7.   The Master said: "The Way does not prevail. I shall take a raft and put out to sea. I am sure Zilu will accompany me." Hearing this, Zilu was overjoyed. The Master said: "Zilu is bolder than I. Still, where would we get the timber for our craft?"

5.8.   Lord Meng Wu asked the Master if Zilu was good. The Master said: "I do not know." The other asked again. The Master said: "In the government of a middle-sized country, he could be entrusted with the ministry of defense. But whether he is good, I do not know."

"And what about Ran Qiu?" The Master said: "Ran Qiu? He could be the mayor of a small city or the steward of a large estate. But whether he is good, I do not know."

"And what about Gongxi Chi?" The Master said: "Gongxi Chi? Girt with his sash, he could stand at court and entertain distinguished guests. But whether he is good, I do not know."

5.9.   The Master asked Zigong: "Which is the better, you or Yan Hui?"—"How could I compare myself with Yan Hui? From one thing he learns, he deduces ten; from one thing I learn, I only deduce two." The Master said: "Indeed, you are not his equal; and neither am I."

5.10.   Zai Yu was sleeping during the day. The Master said: "Rotten wood cannot be carved; dung walls cannot be troweled. What is the use of scolding him?"

The Master said: "There was a time when I used to listen to what people said and trusted that they would act accordingly, but now I listen to what they say and watch what they do. It is Zai Yu who made me change."

5.11.   The Master said: "I have never seen a man who was truly steadfast." Someone replied: "Shen Cheng?" The Master said: "Shen Cheng is driven by his desires. How could he be called steadfast?"

5.12.   Zigong said: "I would not want to do to others what I do not want them to do to me." The Master said: "Oh, you have not come that far yet!"

5.13.   Zigong said: "Our Master's views on culture can be gathered, but it is not possible to hear his views on the nature of things and on the Way of Heaven."

5.14.   When Zilu had learned one thing, his only fear was that he might learn another one before he had the chance to practice the first.

5.15.   Zigong asked: "Why was Kong-the-Civilized called "Civilized"? The Master said: "Because he had an agile mind, was fond of learning, and was not ashamed to seek enlightenment from his inferiors."

5.16.   The Master said of Zichan: "He followed the way of a gentleman in four respects: in his private conduct he was dignified; in serving his master he was respectful; in caring for the people he was generous; in employing the people he was just."

5.17.   The Master said: "Yan Ying knew the art of social intercourse: with him long acquaintance never turned to familiarity."

5.18.   The Master said: "Zang Sunchen built a house for his tortoise, with pillars in the shape of mountains and rafters decorated with duckweed. Had he lost his mind?"

5.19.   Zizhang asked: "Three times, Ziwen was appointed prime minister, but he never showed any elation. Three times, he was dismissed, but he never showed any disappointment. Each time, he duly briefed his successor on the affairs of his office. What do you say?" The Master said: "He was loyal." Zizhang said: "Was he good?" The Master said: "I do not know; I do not see why we should call him good."

"When Cui Zhu killed the sovereign of Qi, Chen Xuwu, who had a large domain, abandoned his estate and left Qi. Having settled in another country, he said: 'They are no better than Cui Zhu,' and he left. Having settled in yet another country, he said once more: 'They are no better than Cui Zhu,' and left again. What do you say?" The Master said: "He was pure." Zizhang said: "Was he good?" The Master said: "I do not know. I do not see why we should call him good."

5.20.   Lord Ji Wen always thought thrice before acting. Hearing this, the Master said: "Twice is enough."

5.21.   The Master said: "When the Way prevailed in the country, Lord Ning Wu was intelligent. When the country lost the Way, Lord Ning Wu became stupid. His intelligence can be equaled; his stupidity is peerless."

5.22.   The Master was in Chen. He said: "Let us go home, let us go home! Our young people are full of fire, they have brilliant talents, but they do not know yet how to use them."

5.23.   The Master said: "Boyi and Shuqi never remembered old grievances and seldom provoked resentment."

5.24.   The Master said: "Who said that Weisheng Gao was straight? When someone asked him for vinegar, he begged it from his next door neighbor and gave it as his own."

5.25.   The Master said: "Glib talk, affectation, and obsequiousness—Zuoqiu Ming despised these, and I despise them too. To befriend a man one secretly resents—Zuoqiu Ming despised this, and I despise it too."

5.26. Yan Hui and Zilu were in attendance. The Master said: "How about telling me your private wishes?"

Zilu said: "I wish I could share my carriages, horses, clothes, and furs with my friends without being upset when they damage them."

Yan Hui said. "I wish I would never boast of my good qualities or call attention to my good deeds."

Zilu said: "May we ask what are our Master's private wishes?"

The Master said: "I wish the old may enjoy peace, friends may enjoy trust, and the young may enjoy affection."

5.27. The Master said: "Alas, I have never seen a man capable of seeing his own faults and of exposing them in the tribunal of his heart."

5.28. The Master said: "In a hamlet of ten houses, you will certainly find people as loyal and faithful as I, but you will not find one man who loves learning as much as I do."

6.1 The Master said: "Ran Yong has in him the making of a prince."

6.2. Ran Yong asked about Zisang Bosi. The Master said: "His easygoing ways are quite all right." Ran Yong said: "To be strict with oneself but easygoing with the people is acceptable. To be easygoing with oneself and easygoing with the people would be too much laxity. Am I right?" The Master said: "You are right."

6.3. Duke Ai asked: "Which of the disciples has a love of learning?" Confucius replied: "There was Yan Hui who loved learning; he never vented his frustrations upon others; he never made the same mistake twice. Alas, his allotted span of life was short: he is dead. Now, for all I know, there is no one with such a love of learning."

6.4. Gongxi Chi was sent on a mission to Qi. Master Ran Qiu requested an allowance of grain for Gongxi's mother. The Master said: "Give her a potful." He asked for more. The Master said: "Give her one measure." Master Ran Qiu gave her a hundred times more. The Master said: "Gongxi Chi is traveling to Qi with sleek horses and fine furs. I have always heard that a gentleman helps the needy; he does not make the rich richer still."

6.5.   Yuan Xian became Confucius's steward and was offered an allowance of nine hundred measures of grain, but he declined it. The Master said: "Don't! You can give it to the people in your village."

6.6.   The Master said about Ran Yong: "Some might hesitate to select for a sacrifice the offspring of a plough ox; yet, if a young bull has good horns and a sorrel coat, would the Spirits of the Hills and Rivers reject it?"

6.7.   The Master said: "Ah! Yan Hui could attach his mind to goodness for three months without interruption, whereas the others manage this only now and then."

6.8.   Lord Ji Kang asked: "Could Zilu be made a minister?" The Master said: "Zilu is resolute; why not make him a minister?"

The other asked again: "Could Zigong be made a minister?"—"Zigong is sagacious; why not make him a minister?"

The other asked again: "Could Ran Qiu be made a minister?"—"Ran Qiu is talented; why not make him a minister?"

6.9.   The head of the Ji Family invited Min Ziqian to run his estate at Bi. Min Ziqian replied to the messenger: "Kindly convey my regrets. Yet, should a new offer be made, I shall have to withdraw on the other side of the river Wen."

6.10.   Boniu was ill. The Master went to enquire after him. Holding Boniu's hand through the window, he said: "He is lost. Such is fate, alas! That such a man should have an illness like this, that such a man should have an illness like this!"

6.11.   The Master said: "How admirable was Yan Hui! A handful of rice to eat, a gourd of water for drink, a hovel for your shelter—no one would endure such misery, yet Yan Hui's joy remained unaltered. How admirable was Yan Hui!"

6.12. Ran Qiu said: "It is not that I do not enjoy the Master's way, but I do not have the strength to follow it." The Master said: "He who does not have the strength can always give up halfway. But you have given up before starting."

6.13. The Master said to Zixia: "Be a noble scholar, not a vulgar pedant."

6.14. Ziyou was governor of Wucheng. The Master said: "Have you got the right sort of people there?"—"There is one Tantai Mieming: he takes no shortcuts; he has not once come to my house, except on official business."

6.15. The Master said: "Meng Zhifan was no boaster. In a rout, he remained behind to cover the retreat. It was only on reaching the city gate that he spurred his horse and said: "It was not courage that kept me at the rear, but the slowness of my horse."

6.16. The Master said: "To survive in an age like ours, it is not enough to have the beauty of Prince Zhao of Song. One also needs the agile tongue of Priest Tuo."

6.17. The Master said: "Who would leave a house without using the door? Why do people seek to walk outside the Way?"

6.18. The Master said: "When nature prevails over culture, you get a savage; when culture prevails over nature, you get a pedant. When nature and culture are in balance, you get a gentleman."

6.19. The Master said: "A man survives thanks to his integrity. If he survives without it, it is sheer luck."

6.20.   The Master said: "To know something is not as good as loving it; to love something is not as good as rejoicing in it."

6.21.   The Master said: "You can expound superior things to average people; you cannot expound superior things to inferior people."

6.22.   Fan Chi asked about wisdom. The Master said: "Secure the rights of the people; respect ghosts and gods, but keep them at a distance—this is wisdom indeed."

Fan Chi asked about goodness. The Master said: "A good man's trials bear fruit—this is goodness indeed."

6.23.   The Master said: "The wise find joy on the water, the good find joy in the mountains. The wise are active, the good are quiet. The wise are joyful, the good live long."

6.24.   The Master said: "With one reform, the country of Qi could reach the level of Lu; with one reform, Lu could reach the Way."

6.25.   The Master said: "A square vase that is not square— square vase indeed!"

6.26.   Zai Yu asked: "If one were to tell a good man that goodness lies at the bottom of the well, should he jump to join it?" The Master said: "Why should he? A gentleman may be misinformed, he cannot be seduced: he may be deceived, he cannot be led astray."

6.27.   The Master said: "A gentleman enlarges his learning through literature and restrains himself with ritual; therefore, he is not likely to go wrong."

6.28.   The Master went to see Nanzi, the concubine of Duke Ling. Zilu was not pleased. The Master swore: "If I have done wrong, may Heaven confound me! May Heaven confound me!"

6.29. The Master said: "The moral power of the Middle Way is supreme, and yet it is not commonly found among the people anymore."

6.30. Zigong said: "What would you say of a man who showers the people with blessings and who could save the multitude? Could he be called good? The Master said: "What has this to do with goodness? He would be a saint! Even Yao and Shun would be found deficient in this respect. As for the good man: what he wishes to achieve for himself, he helps others to achieve; what he wishes to obtain for himself, he enables others to obtain—the ability simply to take one's own aspirations as a guide is the recipe for goodness."

Chapter

7

7.1. The Master said: "I transmit, I invent nothing. I trust and love the past. In this, I dare to compare myself to our venerable Peng."

7.2. The Master said: "To store up knowledge in silence, to remain forever hungry for learning, to teach others without tiring—all this comes to me naturally."

7.3. The Master said: "Failure to cultivate moral power, failure to explore what I have learned, incapacity to stand by what I know to be right, incapacity to reform what is not good—these are my worries."

7.4. At home, the Master was composed and cheerful.

7.5. The Master said: "I am getting dreadfully old. It has been a long time since I last saw in a dream the Duke of Zhou."

7.6. The Master said: "Set your heart upon the Way; rely upon moral power; follow goodness; enjoy the arts."

7.7. The Master said: "I never denied my teaching to anyone who sought it, even if he was too poor to offer more than a token present for his tuition."

7.8. The Master said: "I enlighten only the enthusiastic; I guide only the fervent. After I have lifted up one corner of a question, if the student cannot discover the other three, I do not repeat."

7.9. When the Master ate next to someone in mourning, he never ate his fill.

7.10. On a day when he had wept, the Master never sang.

7.11. The Master said to Yan Hui: "To come out when needed and to hide when dismissed—only you and I can do this."

Zilu said: "If you had command of the Three Armies, whom would you take as your lieutenant?" The Master said: "For my lieutenant, I would not choose a man who wrestles with tigers or swims across rivers without fearing death. He should be full of apprehension before going into action and always prefer a victory achieved by strategy."

7.12. The Master said: "If seeking wealth were a decent pursuit, I too would seek it, even if I had to work as a janitor. As it is, I'd rather follow my inclinations."

7.13. Matters which the Master approached with circumspection: fasting; war; illness.

7.14. When the Master was in Qi, he heard the Coronation Hymn of Shun. For three months, he forgot the taste of meat. He said: "I never imagined that music could reach such a point."

7.15. Ran Qiu said: "Does our Master support the Duke of Wei?" Zigong said: "Well, I am going to ask him."

Zigong went in and asked Confucius: "What sort of people were Boyi and Shuqi?"—"They were virtuous men of old."—

"Did they complain?"———"They sought goodness, they got goodness. Why should they have complained?"

Zigong left and said to Ran Qiu: "Our Master does not support the Duke of Wei."

7.16. The Master said: "Even though you have only coarse grain for food, water for drink, and your bent arm for a pillow, you may still be happy. Riches and honors without justice are to me as fleeting clouds."

7.17. The Master said: "Give me a few more years; if I can study the *Changes* till fifty, I shall be free from big mistakes."

7.18. Occasions when the Master did not use dialect: when reciting the *Poems* and the *Documents,* and when performing ceremonies. In all these occasions, he used the correct pronunciation.

7.19. The Governor of She asked Zilu about Confucius. Zilu did not reply. The Master said: "Why did you not say 'He is the sort of man who, in his enthusiasm, forgets to eat, in his joy forgets to worry, and who ignores the approach of old age'?"

7.20. The Master said: "For my part, I am not endowed with innate knowledge. I am simply a man who loves the past and who is diligent in investigating it."

7.21. The Master never talked of: miracles; violence; disorders; spirits.

7.22. The Master said: "Put me in the company of any two people at random—they will invariably have something to teach me. I can take their qualities as a model and their defects as a warning."

7.23. The Master said: "Heaven vested me with moral power. What do I have to fear from Huan Tui?"

7.24. The Master said to his disciples: "Friends, do you think I am hiding anything from you? I hide nothing. Whatever I do, I share with you. That's how I am."

7.25. The Master made use of four things in his teaching: literature; life's realities; loyalty; good faith.

7.26. The Master said: "A saint, I cannot hope to meet. I would be content if only I could meet a gentleman."

The Master said: "A perfect man, I cannot hope to meet. I would be content if only I could meet a principled man. When Nothing pretends to be Something, Emptiness pretends to be Fullness, and Penury pretends to be Affluence, it is hard to have principles."

7.27. The Master fished with a line, not with a net. When hunting, he never shot a roosting bird.

7.28. The Master said: "Maybe there are people who can act without knowledge, but I am not one of them. Hear much, pick the best and follow it; see much, and keep a record of it: this is still the best substitute for innate knowledge."

7.29. The people of Huxiang were deaf to all teaching; but a boy came to visit the Master. The disciples were perplexed. The Master said: "To approve his visit does not mean approving what he does besides. Why be so finicky? When a man makes himself clean before a visit, we appreciate his cleanliness, we do not endorse his past or his future."

7.30. The Master said: "Is goodness out of reach? As soon as I long for goodness, goodness is at hand."

7.31.   Chen Sibai asked: "Does your Duke Zhao know the ritual?" Confucius said: "He knows the ritual."

Confucius withdrew. Chen, bowing to Wuma Qi, invited him to come forward and said: "I have heard that a gentleman is never partial. Yet isn't your Master very partial indeed? The Duke took a wife from Wu; but since she belonged to his own clan, he changed her name. If this is to know the ritual, then who does not know the ritual?"

Wuma Qi reported this to Confucius. The Master said: "I am fortunate indeed: whenever I make a mistake, there is always someone to notice it."

7.32.   When the Master was singing in company, if someone sang a piece which he liked, he always asked him to repeat it before joining in.

7.33.   The Master said: "My zeal is as strong as anyone's; but I have not yet succeeded in living nobly."

7.34.   The Master said: "I make no claims to wisdom or to human perfection—how would I dare? Still, my aim remains unflagging and I never tire of teaching people." Gongxi Chi said: "This is precisely what we disciples fail to emulate."

7.35.   The Master was severely ill. Zilu asked leave to pray. The Master said: "Is there such a practice?" Zilu said: "Oh yes, and the invocation goes like this: 'We pray you, Spirits from above and Spirits from below.' " The Master said: "In that case, I have been praying for a long time already."

7.36.   The Master said: "Affluence can lead to arrogance; frugality can lead to stinginess. Be stingy rather than arrogant."

7.37.   The Master said: "A gentleman is easygoing and free; a vulgar man is always tense and fretful."

7.38.   The Master was affable, yet stern; he had authority without being overbearing; he was dignified but easy to approach.

Chapter

8

8.1. The Master said: "Of Taibo, one may truly say that his moral power was supreme. Three times, he renounced dominion over the entire world, without giving the people a chance to praise him."

8.2. The Master said: "Without ritual, courtesy is tiresome; without ritual, prudence is timid; without ritual, bravery is quarrelsome; without ritual, frankness is hurtful. When gentlemen treat their kin generously, common people are attracted to goodness; when old ties are not forgotten, common people are not fickle."

8.3. Master Zeng was ill. He called his disciples and said: "Look at my feet! Look at my hands! It is said in the *Poems:*

> Trembling and shaking,
> As if on the edge of an abyss,
> As if treading on thin ice.

But now, my little ones, I know that I have safely reached port."

8.4. Master Zeng was ill. Lord Mengjing came to visit him. Master Zeng said: "When a bird is about to die, his song is sad; when a man is about to die, his words are true. In following the Way, a gentleman pays special attention to three things: in his attitude, he eschews rashness and arrogance; in his expression, he clings to good faith; in his speech, he eschews vulgarity and nonsense. As to the details of liturgy, leave these to the sextons."

8.5.　Master Zeng said: "Competent, yet willing to listen to the incompetent; talented, yet willing to listen to the talentless; having, yet seeming not to have; full, yet seeming empty; swallowing insults without taking offense—long ago, I had a friend who practiced these things."

8.6.　Master Zeng said: "You can entrust him with the care of a little orphan, you can entrust him with the government of a whole country; when put to the test, he remains steadfast. Is such man a gentleman? He is a gentleman indeed."

8.7.　Master Zeng said: "A scholar must be strong and resolute, for his burden is heavy, and his journey is long. His burden is humanity: is this not heavy? His journey ends only with death: is this not long?"

8.8.　The Master said: "Draw inspiration from the *Poems*; steady your course with the ritual; find your fulfillment in music."

8.9.　The Master said: "You can make the people follow the Way, you cannot make them understand it."

8.10.　The Master said: "Trapped by poverty, a brave man might rebel. Pushed too far, a man without morality might rebel."

8.11.　The Master said: "A man may have the splendid talents of the Duke of Zhou, but if he is arrogant and mean, all his merits count for nothing."

8.12.   The Master said: "A man who can study for three years without giving a thought to his career is hard to find."

8.13.   The Master said: "Uphold the faith, love learning, defend the good Way with your life. Enter not a country that is unstable: dwell not in a country that is in turmoil. Shine in a world that follows the Way; hide when the world loses the Way. In a country where the Way prevails, it is shameful to remain poor and obscure; in a country which has lost the Way, it is shameful to become rich and honored."

8.14.   The Master said: "Do not discuss the policies of an office that is not yours."

8.15.   The Master said: "When Zhi, the music master, is conducting, at the opening passage and the finale of *The Ospreys*, what fullness flows to the ear!"

8.16.   The Master said: "Impetuous, yet insincere; ignorant, yet imprudent; naive, yet unreliable—such people are really beyond my understanding."

8.17.   The Master said: "Learning is like a chase in which, as you fail to catch up, you fear to lose what you have already gained."

8.18.   The Master said: "How sublime were Shun and Yu: they had dominion over all that is under Heaven, and yet were not attached to it."

8.19.   The Master said: "What a great ruler Yao was! How sublime! Heaven alone is great, and Yao followed its model. The people could find no words to praise his bounty. How sublime his achievements, and how splendid his institutions!"

8.20.   Shun ruled the entire world with only five ministers. King Wu said: "I have ten ministers."

Confucius said: "Able people are hard to find: how true! The time of Yao and Shun was supposed to be rich in talent, and yet, Shun found only five ministers; as for King Wu, since one of his ministers was a woman, in fact he merely found nine men. Although the House of Zhou had dominion over two-thirds of the world, it still remained a vassal of Shang. One may truly say that the moral power of Zhou was supreme."

8.21.   The Master said: "In Yu, I find no flaw. He drank and ate a frugal fare, but displayed utter devotion in his offerings to the ghosts and spirits; he wore coarse cloth, but his liturgical vestments were magnificent; his dwelling was modest, and he spent his energy in draining floodwaters. In Yu, I find no flaw."

Chapter 9

9.1. The Master seldom spoke of profit, or fate, or humanity.

9.2. A man from Daxiang said: "Your Confucius is really great! With his vast learning, he has still not managed to excel in any particular field." The Master heard of this and said to his disciples: "Which skill should I cultivate? Shall I take up charioteering? Shall I take up archery? All right, I shall take up charioteering."

9.3. The Master said: "According to ritual, the ceremonial cap should be made of hemp; nowadays it is made of silk, which is more convenient; I follow the general usage. According to ritual, one should bow at the bottom of the steps; nowadays people bow on top of the steps, which is rude. Even though it goes against the general usage, I bow at the bottom of the steps."

9.4. The Master absolutely eschewed four things: capriciousness, dogmatism, willfulness, self-importance.

9.5. The Master was trapped in Kuang. He said: "King Wen is dead; is civilization not resting now on me? If Heaven intends civilization to be destroyed, why was it vested in me? If Heaven does not intend civilization to be destroyed, what should I fear from the people of Kuang?"

9.6.   The Grand Chamberlain asked Zigong: "Is your Master not a saint? But then, why should he also possess so many particular aptitudes?" Zigong replied: "Heaven indeed made him a saint; but he also happens to have many aptitudes."

Hearing of this, the Master said: "The Grand Chamberlain truly knows me. In my youth, I was poor; therefore, I had to become adept at a variety of lowly skills. Does such versatility befit a gentleman? No, it does not."

9.7.   Lao said: "The Master said that his failure in public life forced him to develop various skills."

9.8.   The Master said: "Am I knowledgeable? No. A bumpkin asked me a question, and my mind went blank. Still, I hammered at his problem from all sides, till I worked out something."

9.9.   The Master said: "The Phoenix does not come, the River brings forth no chart. It is all over for me!"

9.10.   Whenever the Master saw someone in mourning, or in ceremonial dress, or when he saw a blind man, even one younger than he was, he always stood up, or respectfully moved aside.

9.11.   Yan Hui said with a sigh: "The more I contemplate it, the higher it is; the deeper I dig into it, the more it resists; I saw it in front of me, and then suddenly it was behind me. Step by step, our Master really knows how to entrap people. He stimulates me with literature, he restrains me with ritual. Even if I wanted to stop, I could not. Just as all my resources are exhausted, the goal is towering right above me; I long to embrace it, but cannot find the way."

9.12.   The Master was very ill. Zilu organized the disciples in a retinue, as if they were the retainers of a lord. During a remission of his illness, the Master said: "Zilu, this farce has lasted long enough. Whom can I deceive with these sham retainers? Can I deceive Heaven? Rather than die amidst retainers, I prefer to die in the arms of my disciples. I may not receive a state funeral, but still I shall not die by the wayside."

9.13. Zigong said: "If you had a precious piece of jade, would you hide it safely in a box, or would you try to sell it for a good price?" The Master said: "I would sell it! I would sell it! All I am waiting for is the right offer."

9.14. The Master wanted to settle among the nine barbarian tribes of the East. Someone said: "It is wild in those parts. How would you cope?" The Master said: "How could it be wild, once a gentleman has settled there?"

9.15. The Master said: "It was only after my return from Wei to Lu that the music was put back in order: court pieces on the one hand, hymns on the other."

9.16. The Master said: "I have never found it difficult to serve my superiors abroad and my elders at home; or to bury the dead with due reverence; or to hold my wine."

9.17. The Master stood by a river and said: "Everything flows like this, without ceasing, day and night."

9.18. The Master said: "I have never seen anyone who loved virtue as much as sex."

9.19. The Master said: "It is like the building of a mound: if you stop before the last basket of earth, it remains forever unfinished. It is like the filling of a ditch: once you have tipped in the first basket, you only need to carry on in order to progress."

9.20. The Master said: "What was unique in Yan Hui was his capacity for attention whenever one spoke to him."

9.21. The Master said of Yan Hui: "Alas, I watched his progress, but did not see him reach the goal."

9.22. The Master said: "There are shoots that bear no flower, and there are flowers that bear no fruit."

9.23. The Master said: "One should regard the young with awe: how do you know that the next generation will not equal the present one? If, however, by the age of forty or fifty, a man has not made a name for himself, he no longer deserves to be taken seriously."

9.24. The Master said: "How could words of admonition fail to win our assent? Yet the main thing should be actually to amend our conduct. How could words of praise fail to delight us? Yet the main thing should be actually to understand their purpose. Some people show delight but no understanding, or they assent without changing their ways—I really don't know what to do with them."

9.25. The Master said: "Put loyalty and trust above everything else; do not befriend your moral inferiors; do not be afraid to correct your mistakes."

9.26. The Master said: "One may rob an army of its commander-in-chief; one cannot deprive the humblest man of his free will."

9.27. The Master said: "Only Zilu can stand in his tattered gown by the side of people wearing fine furs without feeling any embarrassment:

> Without envy and without greed
> He must be a good man."

From then on, Zilu was continually chanting these two lines. The Master said: "Come on, this is not the recipe for perfection."

9.28.   The Master said: "It is in the cold of winter that you see how green the pines and cypresses are."

9.29.   The Master said: "The wise are without perplexity; the good are without sorrow; the brave are without fear."

9.30.   The Master said: "There are people with whom you may share information, but not share the Way. There are people with whom you may share the Way, but not share a commitment. There are people with whom you may share a commitment, but not share counsel."

9.31.

> The cherry tree
> Waves its blossoms.
> It is not that I do not think of you
> But your house is so far away!

The Master said: "He does not really love her; if he did, would he mind the distance?"

Chapter

10

10.1.   In his village, Confucius was unassuming in his manners and spoke with hesitation.

In the ancestral temple and at court, his speech was eloquent yet circumspect.

10.2.   At court, when conversing with the under ministers, he was affable; when conversing with the upper ministers, he was respectful. In front of the ruler, he was humble yet composed.

10.3.   When the ruler ordered him to welcome a guest, he showed gravity and eagerness. Bowing and saluting left and right, his gown followed the movements of his body and, as he rushed forward, his sleeves waved like wings. At the end of the visit, he would always announce: "The guest has departed."

10.4.   When entering the gate of the Duke's palace, he walked in discreetly. He never stood in the middle of the passage, nor did he tread on the threshold.

When he passed in front of the throne, he adopted an expression of gravity, hastened his step, and became as if speechless.

When ascending the steps of the audience hall, he lifted up

the hem of his gown and bowed, as if short of breath; on coming out, after descending the first step, he expressed relief and contentment.

At the bottom of the steps, he moved swiftly, as if on wings. On regaining his place, he resumed his humble countenance.

10.5.   When holding the jade tablet, he bowed as if bending under its weight. He placed his upper hand as for a salute, and his lower hand as for an offering. His expression reflected awe, he walked in short steps following a narrow path,

In the ritual presentation of gifts, his expression was debonair.

At the private audience, he was gay.

10.6.   A gentleman does not wear purple or mauve lapels; red and violet should not be used for daily wear at home.

In the heat of summer, he wears light linen, fine or coarse, but never goes out without putting on a gown.

With a black robe, he wears lambskin; with a white robe, deerskin, with a yellow robe, fox fur.

His indoor fur robe is long, with a shorter right sleeve.

His nightgown is of knee length.

Thick furs of fox and badger are to be used inside the house.

Except when in mourning, he wears all his girdle ornaments.

Apart from his ceremonial robe, which is of one piece, all his clothes are cut and sewn.

At funerals, lambskins and black caps should not be worn.

On New Year's Day, he must attend court in court attire.

10.7.   In periods of abstinence, he wears the purification robe, which is made of coarse linen.

In periods of abstinence, he follows another diet and, at home, does not sit in his usual place.

10.8. Even if his rice is of the finest quality, he does not gorge himself; even if his meat is finely minced, he does not gorge himself.

If the food is mouldy or rancid, if the fish is not fresh, if the meat is spoiled, he does not eat it. If the food has gone off color, he does not eat it. If it smells bad, he does not eat it. If it is badly cooked, he does not eat it. If it is not served at the right time, he does not eat it. If it is not properly cut, he does not eat it. If it is not served in its proper sauce, he does not eat it.

Even if there is plenty of meat, he should not eat more meat than rice.

As regards wine, however, there are no restrictions, as long as he retains a clear head.

He does not consume wine bought from a shop, nor dried meat from the market.

He keeps some ginger on the table through the meal, but uses it in moderation.

10.9. After a state sacrifice, the meat should not be kept overnight. The meat of domestic sacrifices should not be kept more than three days. Beyond the third day, it should not be eaten.

10.10. There should be no conversation during meals, and no talk in bed.

10.11. However coarse the fare, one should pray before every meal, and pray devoutly.

10.12. Do not sit on a mat that is not straight.

10.13. When drinking at a village gathering, one should not leave before the elders.

10.14. When an exorcism was performed in his village, he would attend in his court dress, from the eastern stand.

10.15. When dispatching a message to someone abroad, he would bow twice before sending the messenger on his way.

10.16. Lord Ji Kang sent him some medicine. He bowed and accepted the gift, but said: "As I am not acquainted with this substance, I dare not taste it."

10.17. The stables burned. The Master left court and asked: "Was anyone hurt?" He did not inquire about the horses.

10.18. When the prince sends him a present of cooked food, he must straighten his mat and taste it at once. When the prince sends him a present of raw food, he must cook it and offer it to the ancestors. When the prince gives him a live animal, he must rear it.

When waiting upon the prince at mealtime, as the prince is performing the sacrificial offering, he first tastes the food.

10.19. He fell ill. The Duke came to visit him. He had himself laid with his head to the east, his court dress draped over the bed, and the sash drawn across.

10.20. Whenever the Duke summoned him, he would go without waiting for the horses to be harnessed to his carriage.

10.21. When visiting the grand temple, he inquired about everything.

10.22. A friend died; there was no one to take care of the funeral. He said: "Leave it to me."

10.23. On receiving a present from a friend, be it as considerable as a carriage and horses, he would not bow—unless it was a present of sacrificial meat.

10.24.   In bed, he did not lie stiffly like a corpse; at home, he did not sit stiffly like a guest.

10.25.   Whenever he saw a person who was newly bereaved, even if it was someone he met everyday, he always expressed his distress. Whenever he saw someone with a ceremonial cap, or a blind man, even if he was of lowly condition, he would express respect. When driving, he would bow from his chariot to any passer-by in mourning, even if he was a mere peddler.

When presented with a rare delicacy at a banquet, he would express appreciation and rise to his feet.

A sudden clap of thunder or a violent gale always affected his countenance.

10.26.   When climbing into his chariot, he would always stand and face it straight, then grasp the handrail. In the chariot, he did not look back, nor chat volubly, nor point with the finger.

10.27.   Startled, the bird rose up; it flew off, then alighted again.

It is said: "The hen pheasant on the mountain bridge knows the right moment, knows the right moment!"

Zilu bowed towards the bird, which flapped its wings three times and flew away.

Chapter

11

11.1. The Master said: "Before taking office, commoners must first advance in the knowledge of rites and music, whereas noblemen can leave this for later. If I had to appoint officials, I would choose among the former."

11.2. The Master said: "Of all those who shared my tribulations in Chen and Cai, none is still with me."

11.3. Virtue: Yan Hui, Min Ziqian, Ran Boniu, Ran Yong. Eloquence: Zai Yu, Zigong. Government: Ran Qiu, Zilu. Culture: Ziyou, Zixia.

11.4. The Master said: "Yan Hui is of no help to me: whatever I say pleases him."

11.5. The Master said: "Min Ziqian is such a good son! No one ever disagrees with his parents and his brothers when they praise him."

11.6. Nangong Kuo was fond of repeating:

> A flaw in a white jade scepter can be polished away
> But a flaw in words is irretrievable.

Confucius gave him the daughter of his elder brother in marriage.

11.7.   Lord Ji Kang asked: "Which of your disciples loves learning?" Confucius replied: "There was Yan Hui who loved learning. Alas, his life was short: he is dead, and now there is no one."

11.8.   Yan Hui died. His father, Yan Lu, asked if he could dispose of the Master's carriage to provide for an outer coffin. The Master said: "Talented or not, a son is a son. When Li, my own son, died, he was buried only with a coffin and without an outer coffin. I did not go on foot in order to provide for an outer coffin. Since my rank is right behind the grand officers, it is not proper that I should go on foot."

11.9.   Yan Hui died. The Master said: "Alas! Heaven is destroying me, Heaven is destroying me!"

11.10.   Yan Hui died. The Master wailed wildly. His followers said: "Master, such grief is not proper." The Master said: "In mourning such a man, what sort of grief would be proper?"

11.11.   Yan Hui died. The disciples wanted to give him a grand burial. The Master said: "This is not right."

The disciples gave him a grand burial. The Master said: "Yan Hui treated me as his father, and yet I was not given the chance to treat him as my son. This is not my fault, but yours, my friends."

11.12.   Zilu asked how to serve the spirits and gods. The Master said: "You are not yet able to serve men, how could you serve the spirits?"

Zilu said: "May I ask you about death?" The Master said: "You do not yet know life, how could you know death?"

11.13.   When in attendance by the Master's side, Min Ziqian looked respectful; Zilu looked keen; Ran Qiu and Zigong looked affable. The Master was pleased.

(The Master said:) "A man like Zilu will not die a natural death."

11.14. The people of Lu were rebuilding the Long Treasury. Min Ziqian said: "Why not rebuild it along the old lines? Why change the plan?" The Master said: "This man seldom speaks, but when he speaks he hits the mark."

11.15. The Master said: "What sort of music is Zilu playing in my house?" The disciples ceased to respect Zilu. The Master said: "Zilu has ascended to the hall; he has not yet entered the chamber."

11.16. Zigong asked: "Which is the better: Zizhang or Zixia?" The Master said: "Zizhang overshoots and Zixia falls short." Zigong said: "Then Zizhang must be the better?" The Master said: "Both miss the mark."

11.17. The Head of the Ji Family was richer than a king, and yet Ran Qiu kept pressuring the peasants to make him richer still. The Master said: "He is my disciple no more. Beat the drum, my little ones, and attack him: you have my permission."

11.18. Zigao was stupid; Zeng Shen was slow; Zizhang was extreme; Zilu was wild.

11.19. The Master said: "Yan Hui came close to perfection, and yet he often suffered penury. Zigong did not accept his lot and went into business; his judgment is often right."

11.20. Zizhang asked about The-Way-of-the-Good-Man. The Master said: "It is not an old rut, but it does not lead to the inner chamber either."

11.21. The Master said: "His opinions are sound, I agree; yet is he a gentleman, or is this only a solemn pretense?"

11.22.   Zilu asked: "Should I practice at once what I have just learned?" The Master said: "Your father and your elder brother are still alive; how could you practice at once what you have just learned?"

Ran Qiu asked: "Should I practice at once what I have just learned? The Master said: "Practice it at once."

Gongxi Chi said: "When Zilu asked if he should practice at once what he had just learned, you told him to consult first with his father and elder brother. When Ran Qiu asked if he should practice at once what he had just learned, you told him to practice it at once. I am confused; may I ask you to explain?" The Master said: "Ran Qiu is slow, therefore I push him; Zilu has energy for two, therefore I hold him back."

11.23.   The Master was trapped in Kuang; Yan Hui had fallen behind. When they were eventually reunited, the Master said: "I thought you were dead." Yan Hui said: "While you are alive, how would I dare to die?"

11.24.   Ji Ziran asked: "Could one say that Zilu and Ran Qiu are great ministers?" The Master said: "I thought you were going to ask something interesting, but here you are merely asking about Zilu and Ran Qiu! A great minister is a minister who serves his lord by following the Way, and who resigns as soon as the two are no longer reconcilable. Now, as regards Zilu and Ran Qiu, they might just qualify to fill some cabinet vacancies." Ji Ziran said: "Do you mean that they would simply follow any orders?" The Master said: "Not to the point of murdering their father or their lord."

11.25.   Zilu had Zigao appointed as warden of Bi. The Master said: "You are doing that young man a bad turn." Zilu said: "He will busy himself with the local people and their affairs; he will learn things one does not find in books." The Master said: "It is for this sort of remark that I hate smart wits."

11.26.   Zilu, Zeng Dian, Ran Qiu, and Gongxi Chi were sitting with the Master. The Master said: "Forget for one moment that I am your elder. You often say: 'The world does not recognize our merits.' But, given the opportunity, what would you wish to do?"

Zilu rushed to reply first: "Give me a country not too small, but squeezed between powerful neighbors; it is under attack and in the grip of a famine. Put me in charge: within three years, I would revive the spirits of the people and set them back on their feet."

The Master smiled. "Ran Qiu, what about you?"

The other replied: "Give me a domain of sixty to seventy— or, say, fifty to sixty leagues; within three years I would secure the prosperity of its people. As regards their spiritual well-being, however, this would naturally have to wait for the intervention of a true gentleman."

"Gongxi Chi, what about you?"

"I don't say that I would be able to do this, but I would like to learn: in the ceremonies of the Ancestral Temple, such as a diplomatic conference for instance, wearing chasuble and cap, I would like to play the part of a junior assistant."

"And what about you, Zeng Dian?"

Zeng Dian, who had been softly playing his zithern, plucked one last chord and pushed his instrument aside. He replied: "I am afraid my wish is not up to those of my three companions." The Master said: "There is no harm in that! After all, each is simply confiding his personal aspirations."

"In late spring, after the making of the spring clothes has been completed, together with five or six companions and six or seven boys, I would like to bathe in the River Yi, and then enjoy the breeze on the Rain Dance Terrace, and go home singing." The Master heaved a deep sigh and said: "I am with Dian!"

The three others left; Zeng Dian remained behind and said:

"What did you think of their wishes?" The Master said: "Each simply confided his personal aspirations."

"Why did you smile at Zilu?"

"One should govern a state through ritual restraint; yet his words were full of swagger."

"As for Ran Qiu, wasn't he in fact talking about a full-fledged state?"

"Indeed; have you ever heard of 'a domain of sixty to seventy, or fifty to sixty leagues'?"

"And Gongxi Chi? Wasn't he also talking about a state?"

"A diplomatic conference in the Ancestral Temple! What could it be, if not an international gathering? And if Gongxi Chi were there merely to play the part of a junior assistant, who would qualify for the main role?"

Chapter

12.1. Yan Hui asked about humanity. The Master said: "The practice of humanity comes down to this: tame the self and restore the rites. Tame the self and restore the rites for but one day, and the whole world will rally to your humanity. The practice of humanity comes from the self, not from anyone else."

Yan Hui said: "May I ask which steps to follow?" The Master said: "Observe the rites in this way: don't look at anything improper; don't listen to anything improper; don't say anything improper; don't do anything improper."

Yan Hui said: "I may not be clever, but with your permission, I shall endeavor to do as you have said."

12.2. Ran Yong asked about humanity. The Master said: "When abroad, behave as if in front of an important guest. Lead the people as if performing a great ceremony. What you do not wish for yourself, do not impose upon others. Let no resentment enter public affairs; let no resentment enter private affairs."

Ran Yong said: "I may not be clever, but with your permission I shall endeavor to do as you have said."

12.3. Sima Niu asked about humanity. The Master said: "He who practices humanity is reluctant to speak." The other said: "Reluctant to speak? And you call that humanity?" The Master said: "When the practice of something is difficult, how could one speak about it lightly?"

12.4.   Sima Niu asked: "What is a gentleman?" The Master said: "A gentleman is without grief and without fear." Sima Niu said: "Without grief and without fear? And that makes a gentleman?" The Master said: "His conscience is without reproach. Why should he grieve, what should he fear?"

12.5.   Sima Niu was grieving: "All men have brothers; I alone have none." Zixia said: "I have heard this: life and death are decreed by fate, riches and honors are allotted by Heaven. Since a gentleman behaves with reverence and diligence, treating people with deference and courtesy, all within the Four Seas are his brothers. How could a gentleman ever complain that he has no brothers?"

12.6.   Zizhang asked about clear-sightedness. The Master said: "He who is soaked in slander and deafened with denunciations, and still does not waver, may be called clear-sighted. Actually he may also be called farsighted."

12.7.   Zigong asked about government. The Master said: "Sufficient food, sufficient weapons, and the trust of the people." Zigong said: "If you had to do without one of these three, which would you give up?—"Weapons."—"If you had to do without one of the remaining two, which would you give up?"—"Food; after all, everyone has to die eventually. But without the trust of the people, no government can stand."

12.8.   Ji Zicheng said: "One is a gentleman simply by his nature. What is the use of culture?" Zigong said: "Sir, what you have just said is deplorable indeed. *'A team of four horses cannot catch up with a loose tongue.'* Nature is culture, culture is nature. Without its hair, the skin of a tiger or of a leopard is just the same as that of a dog or of a sheep."

12.9.   Duke Ai asked You Ruo: "The crops have failed; I am running out of supplies. What should I do?" You Ruo replied: "Why not levy a tithe?" Duke Ai said: "Even the double of that would not meet my needs; what could be the use of a mere tithe?" You Ruo replied: "If the people have enough, how could their lord not have enough? If the people do not have enough, how could their lord have enough?"

12.10.   Zizhang asked how to accumulate moral power and how to recognize emotional incoherence. The Master said: "Put loyalty and faith above everything, and follow justice. That is how one accumulates moral power. When you love someone, you wish him to live; when you hate someone, you wish him to die. Now, if you simultaneously wish him to live and to die, this is an instance of incoherence."

> If not for the sake of wealth,
> Then for the sake of change . . .

12.11.   Duke Jing of Qi asked Confucius about government. Confucius replied: "Let the lord be a lord; the subject a subject; the father a father; the son a son." The Duke said: "Excellent! If indeed the lord is not a lord, the subject not a subject, the father not a father, the son not a son, I could be sure of nothing anymore—not even of my daily food."

12.12.   The Master said: "To pass judgment on the mere basis of half the evidence: only Zilu can do that."
    Zilu never slept over a promise.

12.13.   The Master said: "I could adjudicate lawsuits as well as anyone. But I would prefer to make lawsuits unnecessary."

12.14.   Zizhang asked about government. The Master said: "Ponder over it untiringly. Carry it out loyally."

12.15.   The Master said: "A gentleman enlarges his learning through literature and restrains himself with ritual; therefore he is not likely to go wrong."

12.16.   The Master said: "A gentleman brings out the good that is in people, he does not bring out the bad. A vulgar man does the opposite."

12.17.   Lord Ji Kang asked Confucius about government. Confucius replied: "To govern is to be straight. If you steer straight, who would dare not to go straight?"

12.18.   Lord Ji Kang was troubled by burglars. He consulted with Confucius. Confucius replied: "If you yourself were not covetous, they would not rob you, even if you paid them to."

12.19.   Lord Ji Kang asked Confucius about government, saying: "Suppose I were to kill the bad to help the good: how about that?" Confucius replied: "You are here to govern; what need is there to kill? If you desire what is good, the people will be good. The moral power of the gentleman is wind, the moral power of the common man is grass. Under the wind, the grass must bend."

12.20.   Zizhang asked: "When can one say that a scholar has attained superior perception?" The Master said: "It depends: what do you mean by 'perception'?" Zizhang replied: "To be recognized in public life, to be recognized in private life." The Master said: "This is recognition, not perception. To attain perception, a man must be cut from straight timber and love justice, examine men's words and observe their expressions, and bear in mind the necessity of deferring to others. As regards recognition, it is enough to put on an air of virtue while behaving to the contrary. Just keep up an unflappable pretense, and you will certainly achieve recognition in public life, and you will certainly achieve recognition in private life."

12.21.   Fan Chi was taking a walk with Confucius under the Rain Dance Terrace. He said: "May I ask how one can accumulate moral power, neutralize hostility, and recognize emotional incoherence?" The Master said: "Excellent question! Always put the effort before the reward: is this not the way to accumulate moral power? To attack evil in itself and not the evil that is in people: is this not the way to neutralize hostility? To endanger oneself and one's kin in a sudden fit of anger: is this not an instance of incoherence?"

12.22.   Fan Chi asked about humanity. The Master said "Love all men."

He asked about knowledge. The Master said: "Know all men." Fan Chi did not understand. The Master said: "Raise the straight and put them above the crooked, so that they may straighten the crooked."

Fan Chi withdrew. He saw Zixia and asked: "A moment ago, as I was with the Master I asked him about knowledge, and he said: 'Raise the straight and put them above the crooked, so that they may straighten the crooked.' What does this mean?" Zixia said: "Rich words indeed! When Shun ruled the world, choosing among the multitude he raised Gao Yao, and the wicked disappeared. When Tang ruled the world, choosing among the multitude he raised Yi Yin, and the wicked disappeared."

12.23.   Zigong asked how to treat friends. The Master said: "Give them loyal advice and guide them tactfully. If that fails, stop: do not expose yourself to rebuff."

12.24.   Master Zeng said: "A gentleman gathers friends through his culture; and with these friends, he develops his humanity."

13.1. Zilu asked about government. The Master said: "Guide them. Encourage them." Zilu asked him to develop these precepts. The Master said: "Untiringly."

13.2. Ran Yong was steward of the Ji Family. He asked about government. The Master said: "Guide the officials. Forgive small mistakes. Promote men of talent." "How does one recognize that a man has talent and deserves to be promoted?" The Master said: "Promote those you know. Those whom you do not know will hardly remain ignored."

13.3. Zilu asked: "If the ruler of Wei were to entrust you with the government of the country, what would be your first initiative?" The Master said: "It would certainly be to rectify the names." Zilu said: "Really? Isn't this a little farfetched? What is this rectification for?" The Master said: "How boorish can you get! Whereupon a gentleman is incompetent, thereupon he should remain silent. If the names are not correct, language is without an object. When language is without an object, no affair can be effected. When no affair can be effected, rites and music wither. When rites and music wither, punishments and penalties miss their target. When punishments and penalties miss their target, the people do not know where they stand. Therefore, whatever a gentleman conceives of, he must be able to say; and whatever he says, he must be able to do. In the matter of language, a gentleman leaves nothing to chance."

13.4. Fan Chi asked Confucius to teach him agronomy. The Master said: "Better ask an old farmer." Fan Chi asked to be taught gardening. The Master said: "Better ask an old gardener."

Fan Chi left. The Master said: "What a vulgar man! If their betters cultivate the rites, the people will not dare to be disrespectful. If their betters cultivate justice, the people will not dare to be disobedient. If their betters cultivate good faith, the people will not dare to be mendacious. To such a country, people would flock from everywhere with their babies strapped to their backs. What is the use of agronomy?"

13.5. The Master said: "Consider a man who can recite the three hundred *Poems;* you give him an official post, but he is not up to the task; you send him abroad on a diplomatic mission, but he is incapable of simple repartee. What is the use of all his vast learning?"

13.6. The Master said: "He is straight: things work out by themselves, without his having to issue orders. He is not straight: he has to multiply orders, which are not being followed anyway."

13.7. The Master said: "In politics, the states of Lu and Wei are brothers."

13.8. The Master commented on Prince Jing of Wei: "He knows how to live. As he began to have a little wealth, he said 'This is quite adequate.' As his wealth increased, he said 'This is quite comfortable.' When his wealth became considerable, he said 'This is quite splendid.' "

13.9.   The Master was on his way to Wei, and Ran Qiu was driving. The Master said: "So many people!" Ran Qiu said: "Once the people are many, what next should be done?"—"Enrich them."—"Once they are rich, what next should be done?"—"Educate them."

13.10.   The Master said: "If a ruler could employ me, in one year I would make things work, and in three years the results would show."

13.11.   The Master said: " 'When good men have been running the country for a hundred years, cruelty can be overcome, and murder extirpated.' How true is this saying!"

13.12.   The Master said: "Even with a true king, it would certainly take one generation for humanity to prevail."

13.13.   The Master said: "If a man can steer his own life straight, the tasks of government should be no problem for him. If he cannot steer his own life straight, how could he steer other people straight?"

13.14.   Ran Qiu was returning from court. The Master said: "What kept you so long?" The other replied: "There were affairs of state." The Master said: "You mean private affairs. Had there been any affairs of state, even though I am not in office, I would have heard of them."

13.15.   Duke Ding asked: "Is there one single maxim that could ensure the prosperity of a country?" Confucius replied: "Mere words could not achieve this. There is this saying, however: 'It is difficult to be a prince, it is not easy to be a subject.' A maxim that could make the ruler understand the difficulty of his task would come close to ensuring the prosperity of the country."

"Is there one single maxim that could ruin a country?"

Confucius replied: "Mere words could not achieve this. There is this saying, however: 'The only pleasure of being a prince is never having to suffer contradiction.' If you are right and no one contradicts you, that's fine; but if you are wrong and no one contradicts you—is this not almost a case of 'one single maxim that could ruin a country'?"

13.16. The Governor of She asked Confucius about government. The Master said: "Make the local people happy and attract migrants from afar."

13.17. Zixia was Warden of Jufu. He asked about politics. The Master said: "Do not try to hurry things. Ignore petty advantages. If you hurry things, you will not reach your goal. If you pursue petty advantages, larger entreprises will not come to fruition."

13.18. The Governor of She declared to Confucius: "Among my people, there is a man of unbending integrity: when his father stole a sheep, he denounced him." Confucius said: "Among my people, men of integrity do things differently: a father covers up for his son, a son covers up for his father— and there is integrity in what they do."

13.19. Fan Chi asked about humanity. The Master said: "Be courteous in private life; reverent in public life; loyal in personal relations. Even among the barbarians, do not depart from this attitude."

13.20. Zigong asked: "How does one deserve to be called a gentleman?" The Master said: "He who behaves with honor, and, being sent on a mission to the four corners of the world, does not bring disgrace to his lord, deserves to be called a gentleman."

"And next to that, if I may ask?"

"His relatives praise his filial piety and the people of his village praise the way he respects the elders."

"And next to that, if I may ask?"

"His word can be trusted; whatever he undertakes, he brings to completion. In this, he may merely show the obstinacy of a vulgar man; still, he should probably qualify as a gentleman of lower category."

"In this respect, how would you rate our present politicians?"

"Alas! These puny creatures are not even worth mentioning!"

13.21.   The Master said: "If I cannot find people who steer a middle course to associate with, I shall be content with the crazy and the pure. The crazy dare do anything, whereas there are things the pure will never do."

13.22.   The Master said: "The Southerners have a saying: 'A man without constancy would not be fit to make a shaman.' How true!"

On the statement in *The Changes:* "To have moral power without steadfastness exposes one to disgrace," the Master commented: "There is no need to cast a horoscope for someone in that condition."

13.23.   The Master said: "A gentleman seeks harmony, but not conformity. A vulgar man seeks conformity, but not harmony."

13.24.   Zigong asked: "What would you think of a man, if all the people in his village liked him?" The Master said: "This is not enough."—"And what if all the people in the village disliked him?"—"This is not enough. It would be better if the good people in the village were to like him, and the bad people to dislike him."

13.25. The Master said: "It is easy to work for a gentleman, but not easy to please him. Try to please him by immoral means, and he will not be pleased; but he never demands anything that is beyond your capacity. It is not easy to work for a vulgar man, but easy to please him. Try to please him, even by immoral means, and he will be pleased; but his demands know no limits."

13.26. The Master said: "A gentleman shows authority, but no arrogance. A vulgar man shows arrogance, but no authority."

13.27. The Master said. "Firmness, resolution, simplicity, silence—these bring us closer to humanity."

13.28. Zilu asked: "How does one deserve to be called a gentleman?" The Master said: "He who shows exacting attention and cordiality deserves to be called a gentleman. Exacting attention toward his friends, and cordiality toward his brothers."

13.29. The Master said: "The people need to be taught by good men for seven years before they can take arms."

13.30. The Master said: "To send to war a people that has not been properly taught is wasting them."

14.1. Yuan Xian asked about shame. The Master said: "When the Way prevails in the state, serve it. To serve a state that has lost the Way—this is shameful indeed."

"He who has shed ambition, boastfulness, resentment, and covetousness, has he achieved the fullness of humanity?"

The Master said: "He has achieved something difficult; whether it is the fullness of humanity, I do not know."

14.2. The Master said: "A scholar who cares for his material comfort does not deserve to be called a scholar."

14.3. The Master said: "When the Way prevails in the state, speak boldly and act boldly. When the state has lost the Way, act boldly and speak softly."

14.4. The Master said: "A virtuous man is always of good counsel; a man of good counsel is not always virtuous. A good man is always brave; a brave man is not always good."

14.5. Nangong Kuo asked Confucius, saying: "Yi was a good archer, and Ao a good sailor: neither died a natural death. Yu and Ji drove a plough: they inherited the world." The Master made no reply.

Nangong Kuo left. The Master said: "What a gentleman! This man really values virtue!"

14.6.   The Master said: "Gentlemen may not always achieve the fullness of humanity. Small men never achieve the fullness of humanity."

14.7.   The Master said: "Can you spare those whom you love? Can loyalty refrain from admonishing?"

14.8.   The Master said: "Whenever an edict had to be written, Pi Chen made the first draft, Shi Shu revised it, Ziyu, the Master of Protocol, edited it, and Zichan of Dongli added the final polish."

14.9.   Someone asked about Zichan. The Master said: "He was a generous man."
   "And what about Zixi?"
   "Oh, that one, don't even mention him!"
   "And what about Guan Zhong?"
   "What a man! At Pian, he took three hundred households from the fief of Bo. The latter, though reduced to eating coarse food till the end of his days, could never bring himself to utter one word of complaint against him."

14.10.   The Master said: "To be poor without resentment is difficult; to be rich without arrogance is easy."

14.11.   The Master said: "Meng Gongchuo is overqualified for the position of steward in a great family, but not qualified enough for the position of minister in a small state."

14.12.   Zilu asked how to define an "accomplished man." The Master said: "One who has the wisdom of Zang Wuzhong, the detachment of Gongchuo, the valor of Zhuangzi of Bian, the skill of Ran Qiu, and could grace all these qualities with rites and music, might be considered an accomplished man." Then he added: "Nowadays, one may perhaps qualify with less: he who does not lose his sense of justice at the sight of profit, who remains ready to give his life amidst all dangers, and who keeps his word through long tribulations may also be considered an accomplished man."

14.13. The Master asked Gongming Jia about Gongshu Wenzi: "Is it true that your master neither spoke, nor laughed, nor took?" Gongming Jia replied: "Those who told you this exaggerated. My master spoke only at the right time, and thus no one ever thought that he spoke too much; he laughed only when he was merry, and thus no one ever thought that he laughed too much; he took only his just reward, and thus no one ever thought that he took too much." The Master said: "Oh, was that so? Could that really have been so?"

14.14. The Master said: "Zang Wuzhong, having occupied Fang, requested that it be acknowledged by Lu as his hereditary fief. Whatever may be said, I cannot believe that he did not exert pressure upon his lord."

14.15. The Master said: "Duke Wen of Jin was subtle but not straight; Duke Huan of Qi was straight, but not subtle."

14.16. Zilu said: "When Duke Huan killed Prince Jiu, one of the Prince's tutors, Shao Hu, died with him, but the other, Guan Zhong, chose to live. Should we say that Guan Zhong's human quality was deficient?" The Master said: "If Duke Huan was able to bring all the states together nine times, it was not through the force of his armies, but thanks to Guan Zhong's authority. Such was his quality, such was his quality!"

14.17. Zigong said: "Guan Zhong, was he not a man without principles? After Duke Huan killed Prince Jiu, not only did he choose to live, but he became a minister of the murderer." The Master said: "By serving as Duke Huan's minister, Guan Zhong imposed his authority over all the states and set the

entire world in order; to this very day, the people still reap
the benefits of his initiatives. Without Guan Zhong, we would
be nothing but disheveled savages who fold their robes on the
wrong side. Now, would you prefer that, like any common
wretch at his wits' end, he had hung himself at the corner of
a ditch, and disappeared without anyone taking the slightest
notice?"

14.18. Zhuan, the steward of Gongshu Wenzi, thanks to his
master, was promoted together with him to the position of
minister. The Master heard this and said: "Gongshu truly
deserved his posthumous title 'The Civilized.'"

14.19. The Master said that Duke Ling of Wei was without
principles. Lord Kang asked: "If this is the case, how is it he
has not lost his state?" Confucius said: "He has Kong Yu in
charge of foreign affairs, Priest Tuo in charge of the ancestors
cult, and Wangsun Jia in charge of defense. Under such conditions, how can he lose his state?"

14.20. The Master said: "A promise easily made is hard to
keep."

14.21. Chen Heng killed Duke Jian of Qi. Confucius made a
ritual ablution and went to court; he told Duke Ai of Lu:
"Chen Heng has killed his prince. Please, punish him." The
Duke said: "Report to the Three Lords."

Confucius said: "It is because I have an official rank that I
felt obliged to make this report. And yet my prince only said:
'Report to the Three Lords.'"

He went and reported to the Three Lords. They refused to
intervene.

Confucius said: "It is because I have an official rank that I
felt obliged to make this report."

14.22.   Zilu asked how to serve a prince. The Master said: "Tell him the truth even if it offends him."

14.23.   The Master said: "A gentleman reaches up. A vulgar man reaches down."

14.24.   The Master said: "In the old days, people studied to improve themselves. Now they study in order to impress others."

14.25.   Qu Boyu sent a messenger to Confucius. Confucius offered him a seat and asked: "How is your master?" The other replied: "My master wishes to make fewer mistakes, but he has not succeeded yet."

The messenger left. The Master said: "What a messenger! What a messenger!"

14.26.   The Master said: "He who holds no official position discusses no official policies."

Master Zeng said: "No gentleman would ever contemplate overstepping his position."

14.27.   The Master said: "A gentleman would be ashamed should his deeds not match his words."

14.28.   The Master said: "A gentleman abides by three principles which I am unable to follow: his humanity knows no anxiety; his wisdom knows no hesitation; his courage knows no fear." Zigong said: "Master, you have just drawn your own portrait."

14.29.   Zigong was criticizing other people. The Master said: "Zigong must have already reached perfection, which affords him a leisure I do not possess."

14.30.   The Master said: "It is not your obscurity that should distress you, but your incompetence."

14.31.   The Master said: "Without anticipating deception or suspecting bad faith, still to be able to detect them at once, is sagacity indeed."

14.32.   Weisheng Mu said to Confucius: "Hey, you!, what makes you run around like this all the time? Is it to show off your clever tongue?" Confucius said: "I don't flatter myself with having a clever tongue; I simply detest pigheadedness."

14.33.   The Master said: "The famous horse Ji was valued not for its physical strength, but for its inner force."

14.34.   Someone said: "To repay hatred with kindness—what do you think of that?" The Master said: "And what will you repay kindness with? Rather repay hatred with justice, and kindness with kindness."

14.35.   The Master said: "No one understands me!" Zigong said: "Why is it that no one understands you?" The Master said: "I do not accuse Heaven, nor do I blame men; here below I am learning, and there above I am being heard. If I am understood, it must be by Heaven."

14.36.   Gongbo Liao slandered Zilu to Ji Sun. Zifu Jingbo reported this to Confucius, saying: "My master's mind is being swayed by Gongbo Liao; but I still have the power to get his carcass exposed in the marketplace." The Master said: "If it is Heaven's will, the truth will prevail; if it is Heaven's will, the truth will perish. What does Gongbo Liao matter set against Heaven's will?"

14.37.   The Master said: "The highest wisdom is to avoid the world; next, to avoid certain places; next, to avoid certain attitudes; next, to avoid certain words."   .

   The Master said: "Seven men did this."

14.38.   Zilu stayed for the night at the Stone Gate. The gate-keeper said: "Where are you from?" Zilu said: "I am from Confucius's household."—"Oh, is that the one who keeps pursuing what he knows is impossible?"

14.39.   The Master was playing the stone chimes in Wei. A man carrying a basket passed in front of his gate and said: "He puts real heart in his music!" A little later, however, he added: "How mean, this little jingle! If the world ignores you, so be it!

> If the water of the ford is deep, wade through it with your
> clothes on;
> If the water is shallow, lift up the hem of your gown."

The Master said: "How bold! I am speechless."

14.40.   Zizhang said: "In the *Documents*, it is written: 'When King Gaozong was mourning his father, he did not speak for three years.' What does that mean?" The Master said: "There is no need to single out the case of King Gaozong, all the ancients did the same. During the three years following the death of a ruler, all the officials who had been appointed by him remained in place, taking their orders from his prime minister."

14.41.   The Master said: "When their betters cultivate civility, the people are easily led."

14.42.   Zilu asked what makes a gentleman. The Master said: "Through self-cultivation, he achieves dignity.—"Is that all?"—"Through self-cultivation, he spreads his peace to his neighbors."—"Is that all?"—"Through self-cultivation, he spreads his peace to all the people. Through self-cultivation, to spread one's peace to all the people: even Yao and Shun could not have aimed for more."

14.43. Yuan Rang sat waiting, with his legs spread wide. The Master said: "A youth who does not respect his elders will achieve nothing when he grows up, and will even try to shirk death when he reaches old age: he is a parasite." And he struck him across the shin with his stick.

14.44. A boy from the village of Que was employed as his messenger. Someone enquired about him, saying: "Is he making any progress?" The Master said: "From what I see, watching him as he grabs a seat for himself, or walks alongside people older than himself, what interests him, it seems, is not how to progress, but how to arrive quickly."

Chapter

15

15.1. Duke Ling of Wei asked Confucius about military tactics. Confucius replied: "I do have some experience in the handling of ritual vessels, but I never learned how to handle troops." He left the next day.

15.2. In Chen, he ran out of supplies. His followers became weak: they could no longer rise to their feet. Zilu came to see him and said indignantly: "How is it possible for a gentleman to find himself in such distress?" The Master said: "A gentleman can indeed find himself in distress, but only a vulgar man is upset by it."

15.3. The Master said: "Zigong, do you think that I am someone who learns a lot of things and then stores them all up?"—"Indeed; is it not so?" The Master said: "No. I have one single thread on which to string them all."

15.4. The Master said: "Zilu, how rare are those who understand moral power."

15.5. The Master said: "Shun was certainly one of those who knew how to govern by inactivity. How did he do it? He sat reverently on the throne, facing south—and that was all."

15.6. Zizhang asked about conduct. The Master said: "Speak with loyalty and good faith, act with dedication and deference, and even among the barbarians your conduct will be irreprochable. If you speak without loyalty and good faith, if you act without dedication or deference, your conduct will be unacceptable, even in your own village. Wherever you stand, you should have this precept always in front of your eyes; have it carved upon the yoke of your chariot, and only then will you be able to move ahead." Zizhang wrote it on his sash.

15.7. The Master said: "How straight Shi Yu was! Under a good government, he was straight as an arrow; under a bad government, he was straight as an arrow. What a gentleman was Qu Boyu! Under a good government, he displayed his talents. Under a bad government, he folded them up in his heart."

15.8. The Master said: "When dealing with a man who is capable of understanding your teaching, if you do not teach him, you waste the man. When dealing with a man who is incapable of understanding your teaching, if you do teach him, you waste your teaching. A wise teacher wastes no man and wastes no teaching."

15.9. The Master said: "A righteous man, a man attached to humanity, does not seek life at the expense of his humanity; there are instances where he will give his life in order to fulfill his humanity."

15.10. Zigong asked how to practice humanity. The Master said: "A craftman who wishes to do good work must first sharpen his tools. In whatever country you may settle, offer your services to the most virtuous ministers and befriend those gentlemen who cultivate humanity."

15.11. Yan Hui asked how to govern a state. The Master said: "Observe the calendar of Xia; ride in the chariot of Yin;

wear the cap of Zhou. As for music, follow the Coronation Hymn of Shun and the Victory Hymn of Wu. Proscribe the music of Zheng. Stay away from clever talkers. The music of Zheng corrupts. Clever talkers are dangerous."

15.12.   The Master said: "A man with no concern for the future is bound to worry about the present."

15.13.   The Master said: "The fact remains that I have never seen a man who loved virtue as much as sex."

15.14.   The Master said: "Zang Sunchen stole his office! He knew that Liuxia Hui was better qualified, and yet he did not share his position with him."

15.15.   The Master said: "Demand much from yourself, little from others, and you will prevent discontent."

15.16.   The Master said: "With those who cannot say 'What should I do? what should I do?,' I really do not know what I should do."

15.17.   The Master said: "I cannot abide these people who are capable of spending a whole day together in a display of wits without ever hitting upon one single truth."

15.18.   The Master said: "A gentleman takes justice as his basis, enacts it in conformity with the ritual, expounds it with modesty, and through good faith, brings it to fruition. This is how a gentleman proceeds."

15.19.   The Master said: "A gentleman resents his incompetence; he does not resent his obscurity."

15.20.   The Master said: "A gentleman worries lest he might disappear from this world without having made a name for himself."

15.21. The Master said: "A gentleman makes demands on himself; a vulgar man makes demands on others."

15.22. The Master said: "A gentleman is proud without being aggressive, sociable but not partisan."

15.23. The Master said: "A gentleman does not approve of a person because he expresses a certain opinion, nor does he reject an opinion because it is expressed by a certain person."

15.24. Zigong asked: "Is there any single word that could guide one's entire life?" The Master said: "Should it not be *reciprocity?* What you do not wish for yourself, do not do to others."

15.25. The Master said: "In my dealings with people, do I ever praise anyone, do I ever blame anyone? If I praise anyone, it is only after having tested him. The people of today are still the same people who once enabled the Three Dynasties to steer a straight course."

15.26. The Master said: "I can still remember that there was a time when scribes encountering a doubtful word would leave a blank space, and horse owners would have their new horses tested by an expert. Nowadays these practices are not followed anymore."

15.27. The Master said: "Clever talk ruins virtue. Small impatiences ruin great plans."

15.28. The Master said: "When everyone dislikes a man, one should investigate. When everyone likes a man, one should investigate."

15.29. The Master said: "Man can enlarge the Way. It is not the Way that enlarges man."

15.30. The Master said: "A fault that is not amended is a fault indeed."

15.31. The Master said: "In an attempt to meditate, I once spent a whole day without food and a whole night without sleep: it was no use. It is better to study."

15.32. The Master said: "A gentleman seeks the Way, he does not seek a living. Plough the fields and perchance you may still go hungry. Apply yourself to learning and perchance you may yet make a career. A gentleman worries whether he will find the Way, he does not worry that he may remain poor."

15.33. The Master said: "The power that can be attained through knowledge but cannot be retained through goodness will certainly be lost in the end. The power that is attained through knowledge and retained through goodness will still not be respected by the people if it is not exerted with dignity. The power that is attained through knowledge, retained through goodness, and exerted with dignity, if it is not wielded in accordance with the ritual, is still not the right sort of power."

15.34. The Master said: "A gentleman's ability cannot be seen in small matters; yet he can be entrusted with great tasks. A vulgar man cannot be entrusted with great tasks, but his ability can be seen in small matters."

15.35. The Master said: "Humanity is more essential to the people than water and fire. I have seen men lose their lives by surrendering themselves to water or fire; I never saw anyone lose his life by surrendering himself to humanity."

15.36. The Master said: "In the pursuit of virtue, do not be afraid to overtake your teacher."

15.37. The Master said: "A gentleman is principled but not rigid."

15.38. The Master said: "In serving the prince, devotion to one's duty should come before any thought of reward."

15.39. The Master said: "My teaching is addressed to all indifferently."

15.40. The Master said: "With those who follow a different Way, to exchange views is pointless."

15.41. The Master said: "Words are merely for communication."

15.42. Mian, the blind music master, came to visit. When he reached the steps, the Master said: "Mind the steps." Taking him to his seat, the Master said: "Here is your seat." When everyone was seated, the Master explained: "So-and-so is here, So-and-so is there."

After the music master had left, Zizhang asked: "Is this the way to address a musician?" The Master said: "Yes; this is the way to guide a musician."

Chapter

16

16.1. Lord Ji was going to attack Zhuanyu. Ran Qiu and Zilu came to see Confucius, and said to him: "Lord Ji is going to intervene in Zhuanyu."

Confucius said: "Qiu, is it not you who should be blamed for this? Our ancient kings established Zhuanyu as an autonomous domain; moreover, it is at the heart of our territory; it is paying allegiance to us. Why attack it?"

Ran Qiu said: "It is our master's wish, it is not the wish of either of us."

Confucius said: "Qiu! Zhou Ren said, 'He who has the strength stands firm; he who feels inadequate withdraws.' What sort of assistant is he, who cannot steady his master when he totters, nor support him when he trips? Moreover, what you said is wrong. If a tiger or a rhinoceros escapes from its cage, if a tortoise shell or a jade is broken in its casket, should no one be accountable for the mishap?"

Ran Qiu said: "Now Zhuanyu has strong defenses and is close to our master's castle. If he does not take it today, in the future it will become a menace for his children and grandchildren."

Confucius said: "Qiu! A gentleman abhors those people who invent excuses for their actions instead of stating plainly: 'I want this.' I have always heard that what worries the head of a state or the chief of a clan is not poverty but inequality, not the lack of population, but the lack of peace. For if there is equality, there will be no poverty, and where there is peace, there is no lack of population. And then, if people who live in far-off lands still resist your attraction, you must draw them to you by the moral power of civilization; and then, having attracted them, make them enjoy your peace. But now, with you two as his ministers, your master is incapable of attracting people from far away, his land is racked with divisions and unrest, he cannot hold it together any longer—and yet he wants to wage war against one of his own provinces! For Lord Ji, I am afraid, the real menace does not come from Zhuanyu, it lies within the walls of his own palace."

16.2. Confucius said: "When the world follows the Way, rites, music, and military expeditions are all determined by the Son of Heaven. When the world has lost the Way, rites, music, and military expeditions are all determined by the feudal lords. Once it is the feudal lords who determine these matters, their authority seldom lasts for ten generations; once it is their ministers who determine these matters, their authority seldom lasts for five generations; once the affairs of the country fall into the hands of the stewards of the ministers their authority seldom lasts for three generations. In a world which follows the Way, political initiative does not belong to the ministers; in a world which follows the Way, there is no need for commoners to dispute over politics."

16.3. Confucius said: "The Ducal House of Lu has lost its authority for five generations already; political power has fallen into the hands of the ministers for four generations already; therefore, the future of their descendants is now precarious."

16.4.   Confucius said: "Three sorts of friends are beneficial; three sorts of friends are harmful. Friendship with the straight, the trustworthy, and the learned is beneficial. Friendship with the devious, the obsequious, and the glib is harmful."

16.5.   Confucius said: "Three sorts of pleasure are profitable; three sorts of pleasure are harmful. The pleasure of performing rites and music properly, the pleasure of praising other people's qualities, the pleasure of having many talented friends is profitable. The pleasure of extravagant display, the pleasure of idle wandering, the pleasure of lewd carousing is harmful."

16.6.   Confucius said: "When waiting upon a gentleman, one should avoid three mistakes. To speak before having been invited to do so—this is rashness. Not to speak when invited to do so—this is secretiveness. To speak without observing the gentleman's expression—this is blindness."

16.7.   Confucius said: "A gentleman must guard himself against three dangers. When young, as the energy of the blood is still in turmoil, he should guard against lust. In his maturity, as the energy of the blood is at its full, he should guard against rage. In old age, as the energy of the blood is on the wane, he should guard against rapacity."

16.8.   Confucius said: "A gentleman fears three things. He fears the will of Heaven. He fears great men. He fears the words of the saints. A vulgar man does not fear the will of Heaven, for he does not know it. He despises greatness and he mocks the words of the saints."

16.9.   Confucius said: "Those who have innate knowledge are the highest. Next come those who acquire knowledge through learning. Next again come those who learn through the trials of life. Lowest are the common people who go through the trials of life without learning anything."

16.10. Confucius said: "A gentleman takes care in nine circumstances:
    —when looking, to see clearly;
    —when listening, to hear distinctly;
    —in his expression, to be amiable;
    —in his attitude, to be deferential;
    —in his speech, to be loyal;
    —when on duty, to be respectful;
    —when in doubt, to question;
    —when angry, to ponder the consequences;
    —when gaining an advantage, to consider if it is fair."

16.11. Confucius said: " 'Thirst for goodness; recoil from evil': I have heard this saying, and I have seen it practiced. 'Withdraw from the world and pursue the aspirations of your heart; walk in righteousness to reach the Way': I have heard this saying, but I have never seen it practiced."

16.12. Duke Jing of Qi had a thousand chariots of war. On the day of his death, the people could not find anything for which to praise his memory. Boyi and Shuqi starved in the wilderness; to this very day, the people are still celebrating their merits. Is this not an illustration of what was just said?"

16.13. Chen Ziqin asked Confucius's son: "Have you received any special teaching from your father?" The other replied: "No. Once, as he was standing alone, and I was discreetly crossing the courtyard, he asked me: 'Have you studied the *Poems?*' I replied: 'No.' He said: 'If you do not study the *Poems,* you will not be able to hold your own in any discussion.' I withdrew and studied the *Poems.* Another day, as he was again standing alone and I was discreetly crossing the courtyard, he asked me: 'Have you studied the ritual?' I replied: 'No.' IIe said: 'If you do not study the ritual, you will not be able to take your stand in society.' I withdrew and studied the ritual. These are the two teachings I received."

Chen Ziqin went away delighted and said: "I asked one thing, and learned three. I learned about the *Poems,* I learned about the ritual, and I learned how a gentleman maintains distance from his son."

16.14. Various titles are used for the consort of a ruler. The ruler calls her 'My Lady.' She calls herself 'Your little maid.' The people call her 'The Lord's Lady,' but when talking to foreigners, they refer to her as 'Our little sovereign.' Foreigners also call her 'The Lord's Lady.'

17.1.   Yang Huo wanted to see Confucius. Confucius would not see him. Yang Huo sent him a suckling pig. Confucius chose a time when the other was not at home, and called to acknowledge the present. They met on the road.

Yang Huo said to Confucius: "Come! I have something to tell you." He went on: "Can a man be called virtuous if he keeps his talents for himself while his country is going astray? I do not think so. Can a man be called wise if he is eager to act, yet misses every opportunity to do so? I do not think so. The days and months go by, time is not with us."

Confucius said: "All right, I shall accept an office."

17.2.   The Master said: "What nature put together, habit separates."

17.3.   The Master said: "Only the wisest and the stupidest never change."

17.4.   The Master went to Wucheng, where Ziyou was governor. He heard the sound of stringed instruments and hymns. He was amused and said with a smile: "Why use an ox-cleaver to kill a chicken?" Ziyou replied: "Master, in the past I have heard you say: 'The gentleman who cultivates the Way loves all men; the small people who cultivate the Way are easy to govern.'" The Master said: "My friends, Ziyou is right. I was just joking."

17.5. Gongshan Furao, who was holding the fortress of Bi, rebelled and invited Confucius to join him: The Master was tempted to go. Zilu was dismayed by this, and said: "It is too bad if we have nowhere to go, but is this a reason to join Gongshan?" The Master said: "Since he is inviting me, it must be for some purpose. If only someone would employ me, I could establish a new Zhou dynasty in the East."

17.6. Zizhang asked Confucius about humanity. The Master said: "Whoever could spread the five practices everywhere in the world would implement humanity." "And what are these?" "Courtesy, tolerance, good faith, diligence, generosity. Courtesy wards off insults; tolerance wins all hearts; good faith inspires the trust of others; diligence ensures success; generosity confers authority upon others."

17.7. Bi Xi invited Confucius. The Master was tempted to go. Zilu said: "Master, in the past I heard you say 'A gentleman does not associate with those who are personally committing evil.' Bi Xi is making use of his stronghold of Zhongmou to start a rebellion. How can you contemplate joining him?" The Master said. "Indeed, I said that. And yet what resists grinding is truly strong, what resists black dye is truly white. Am I a bitter gourd, good only to hang as decoration, but unfit to be eaten?"

17.8. The Master said: "Zilu, have you heard of the six qualities and their six perversions?"—"No."—"Sit down, I will tell you. The love of humanity without the love of learning degenerates into silliness. The love of intelligence without the love of learning degenerates into frivolity. The love of chivalry without the love of learning degenerates into banditry. The love of frankness without the love of learning degenerates into brutality. The love of valor without the love of learning degenerates into violence. The love of force without the love of learning degenerates into anarchy."

17.9. The Master said: "Little ones, why don't you study the *Poems?* The *Poems* can provide you with stimulation and with observation, with a capacity for communion, and with a vehicle for grief. At home, they enable you to serve your father, and abroad, to serve your lord. Also, you will learn there the names of many birds, animals, plants, and trees."

17.10. The Master said to his son: "Have you worked through the first and the second part of the *Poems?* Whoever goes into life without having worked through the first and the second part of the *Poems* will remain stuck, as if facing a wall."

17.11. The Master said. "They speak of the rites here, and the rites there—as if ritual merely meant offerings of jade and silk! They speak of music here, and music there—as if music merely meant bells and drums!"

17.12. The Master said: "A coward who assumes fierce looks is—to borrow a crude image—like a cutpurse who sneaks over a wall."

17.13. The Master said: "Those who make virtue their profession are the ruin of virtue."

17.14. The Master said: "Peddlers of hearsay are virtue's derelicts."

17.15. The Master said: "Can one serve a prince in the company of a cad? Before he gets his position, his only fear is that he might not get it, and once he gets it, his only fear is that he might lose it. And when he fears to lose it, he becomes capable of anything."

17.16. The Master said: "The ancients had three faults, which moderns are not even capable of. The eccentricity of the ancients was carefree, whereas modern eccentricity is licentious. The pride of the ancients was blunt, whereas modern pride is cantankerous. The naiveté of the ancients was straight, whereas modern naiveté is an imposture."

17.17. The Master said: "Clever talk and affected manners are seldom signs of goodness."

17.18. The Master said: "I detest purple replacing vermilion; I detest popular music corrupting classical music; I detest glib tongues overturning kingdoms and clans."

17.19. The Master said: "I wish to speak no more." Zigong said: "Master, if you do not speak, how would little ones like us still be able to hand down any teachings?" The Master said: "Does Heaven speak? Yet the four seasons follow their course and the hundred creatures continue to be born. Does Heaven speak?"

17.20. Ru Bei wanted to see Confucius. Confucius declined on the grounds of illness. As Ru Bei's messenger was leaving, the Master took up his zithern and sang loudly enough for him to hear.

17.21. Zai Yu asked: "Three years mourning for one's parents—this is quite long. If a gentleman stops all ritual practices for three years, the practices will decay; if he stops all musical performances for three years, music will be lost. As the old crop is consumed, a new crop grows up, and for lighting the fire, a new lighter is used with each season. One year of mourning should be enough." The Master said: "If after only one year, you were again to eat white rice and to wear silk, would you feel at ease?"—"Absolutely."—"In that case, go ahead! The reason a gentleman prolongs his mourning is simply that, since fine food seems tasteless to him, and music offers him no enjoyment, and the comfort of his house makes him uneasy, he prefers to do without all these pleasures. But now, if you can enjoy them, go ahead!"

Zai Yu left. The Master said: "Zai Yu is devoid of humanity. After a child is born, for the first three years of his life, he does not leave his parents' bosom. Three years mourning is a custom that is observed everywhere in the world. Did Zai Yu never enjoy the love of his parents, even for three years?"

17.22.   The Master said: "I cannot abide these people who fill their bellies all day long, without ever using their minds! Why can't they play chess? At least it would be better than nothing."

17.23.   Zilu said: "Does a gentleman prize courage?" The Master said: "A gentleman puts justice above everything. A gentleman who is brave but not just may become a rebel; a vulgar man who is brave but not just may become a bandit."

17.24.   Zigong said: "Does a gentleman have hatreds?" The Master said: "Yes. He hates those who dwell on what is hateful in others. He hates those inferiors who slander their superiors. He hates those whose courage is not tempered by civilized manners. He hates the impulsive and the stubborn." He went on: "And you? Don't you have your own hatreds?"—"I hate the plagiarists who pretend to be learned. I hate the arrogant who pretend to be brave. I hate the malicious who pretend to be frank."

17.25.   The Master said: "Women and underlings are especially difficult to handle: be friendly, and they become familiar; be distant, and they resent it."

17.26.   The Master said: "Whoever, by the age of forty, is still disliked, will remain so till the end."

Chapter 18

18.1. The Lord of Wei fled from the tyrant, the Lord of Ji was enslaved by him, and Bi Gan was executed for remonstrating with him. Confucius said: "The Yin Dynasty had three models of humanity."

18.2. Liuxia Hui was a magistrate. He was dismissed three times. People said: "Why can't you go elsewhere?" He replied: "If I work honestly, where would I not meet the same fate? If I am going to work against my conscience, why should I need to leave the land of my parents?"

18.3. Duke Jing of Qi had invited Confucius. He said: "I cannot treat him on the same footing as Lord Ji. I shall treat him as if his rank were between that of Lord Ji and Lord Meng." Then he said again: "I am too old. I cannot employ him." Confucius left.

18.4. The people of Qi sent to Lu a present of singing and dancing girls. Lord Ji Huan accepted them and, for three days, he did not attend court. Confucius left.

18.5. Jieyu, the Madman of Chu, went past Confucius, singing:

> Phoenix, oh Phoenix!
> The past cannot be retrieved,

> But the future still holds a chance.
>   Give up, give up!
> The days of those in office are numbered!

Confucius stopped his chariot, for he wanted to speak with him, but the other hurried away and disappeared. Confucius did not succeed in speaking to him.

18.6. Changju and Jieni were ploughing together. Confucius, who was passing by, sent Zilu to ask where the ford was. Changju said: "Who is in the chariot?" Zilu said: "It is Confucius." "The Confucius from Lu?"—"Himself."—"Then he already knows where the ford is."

Zilu then asked Jieni, who replied: "Who are you?"—"I am Zilu."—"The disciple of Confucius, from Lu?"—"Yes."—"The whole universe is swept along by the same flood; who can reverse its flow? Instead of following a gentleman who keeps running from one patron to the next, would it not be better to follow a gentleman who has forsaken the world?" All the while he kept on tilling his field.

Zilu came back and reported to Confucius. Rapt in thought, the Master sighed: "One cannot associate with birds and beasts. With whom should I keep company, if not with my own kind? If the world were following the Way, I would not have to reform it."

18.7. Traveling with Confucius, Zilu fell behind. He met an old man who was carrying on his shoulder a basket hanging from his staff.

Zilu asked him: "Sir, have you seen my master?" The old man said: "You do not toil with your four limbs, you cannot even distinguish between the five sorts of grain—who can be your master?" He planted his staff in the ground and started weeding.

Zilu watched him respectfully.

The old man kept him for the night, killed a chicken, cooked some millet, and presented his two sons to him.

The next day, Zilu resumed his journey and reported to Confucius.

The Master said: "The man you met is a hermit." He sent Zilu back to seek for him, but on arriving at his place, Zilu found that the old man was gone.

Zilu said: "It is not right to withdraw from public life. One cannot ignore the difference between age and youth, and even less the mutual obligations between prince and subject. One cannot discard the most essential human relationships, simply to preserve one's purity. A gentleman has a moral obligation to serve the state, even if he can foresee that the Way will not prevail."

18.8.   Those who withdrew from the world: Boyi, Shuqi, Yuzhong, Yiyi, Zhuzhang, Liuxia Hui, Shaolian. The Master said: "Never compromise, accept no insult—this might sum up the attitude of Boyi and Shuqi." On Liuxia Hui and Shaolian he commented: "They compromised and they suffered insults; still, they succeeded in preserving decency in their words, and prudence in their deeds." On Yuzhong and Yiyi, he commented: "They became hermits and gave up speech. They remained pure, and were shrewd in their self-effacement. As for me, I do things differently: I follow no rigid prescriptions on what should, or should not, be done."

18.9.   Zhi, the grand music master, left for Qi. Gan, musician of the second banquet, left for Chu. Liao, musician of the third banquet, left for Cai. Que, musician of the fourth banquet, left for Qin. The drummer Fangshu crossed the Yellow River. The kettle-drummer Wu crossed the Han River. Yang, the deputy music master, and Xiang, who played the stone chimes, crossed the sea.

18.10.   The Duke of Zhou said to his son, the Duke of Lu: "A gentleman does not neglect his relatives. He does not give his ministers the opportunity to complain of not being trusted. Without serious cause, he does not dismiss old retainers. He does not expect perfection from any single individual."

18.11.   The Zhou Dynasty had eight knights: the elder brothers Da and Gua; the second brothers Tu and Hu, the younger brothers Ye and Xia; the youngest brothers Sui and Gua.

Chapter

19

19.1.   Zizhang said: "Facing danger, a gentleman is ready to give his life; a prospect of profit does not make him forget what is right; when he sacrifices, it is with piety; when he mourns, it is with grief—what more could be desired?"

19.2.   Zizhang said: "If a man embraces virtue without much conviction and follows the Way without much determination, should we really say that he is embracing virtue and following the Way?"

19.3.   The disciples of Zixia asked Zizhang about social intercourse. Zizhang said: "What did Zixia tell you?" They replied: "Zixia said: 'Associate with the right sort of people; avoid those people who are not of the right sort.'" Zizhang said: "I was taught something different: A gentleman respects the wise and tolerates the mediocre; he praises the good and has compassion for the incapable. If I have vast wisdom, whom should I not tolerate? If I do not have vast wisdom, people will avoid me; on what grounds could I avoid them?"

19.4.   Zixia said: "Even minor disciplines have their merits; but he who has a long journey ahead of him fears quagmires, and this is why a gentleman does not enter byways."

19.5.   Zixia said: "He who, day after day, remembers what he still needs to learn and, month after month, does not forget what he has already learned, is truly fond of learning."

19.6.   Zixia said: "Extend your learning and hold fast to your purpose; question closely and meditate on things at hand: there you will find the fullness of your humanity."

19.7.   Zixia said: "The hundred artisans live in their workshops in order to perfect their crafts. A gentleman keeps learning in order to reach the truth."

19.8.   Zixia said: "A vulgar man always tries to cover up his mistakes."

19.9.   Zixia said: "A gentleman produces three different impressions: Look at him from afar: he is stern. Come close: he is amiable. Hear what he says: he is incisive."

19.10.   Zixia said: "A gentleman first wins the trust of his people, and then he can mobilize them. Without this trust, they might feel they are being ill-used. He first wins the trust of his prince, and then he may offer criticism. Without this trust, the prince might feel he is being slandered."

19.11.   Zixia said: "Major principles suffer no transgression. Minor principles may allow for compromise."

19.12.   Ziyou said: "Disciples and young followers of Zixia can manage as long as they are merely required to clean and sweep the floor, to answer the door, to say hello and good-bye. But these are mere trifles. When it comes to fundamental matters, they are completely lost. How is this possible?"

Zixia heard this and said: "No! Ziyou is badly mistaken. In the doctrine of the gentleman, what should be taught first and what is less important? It is like plants and trees: there are many varieties that suit different spots. In the doctrine of the gentleman, how could there be any futility? Only a saint, however, would be able to embrace it from beginning to end."

19.13. Zixia said: "Leisure from politics should be devoted to learning. Leisure from learning should be devoted to politics."

19.14. Ziyou said: "Mourning should express grief, and stop at that."

19.15. Ziyou said: "My friend Zizhang is a man of rare ability, but he has not reached the fullness of humanity."

19.16. Master Zeng said: "Zizhang takes up too much room: it is not easy to cultivate humanity by his side."

19.17. Master Zeng said: "I learned this from the Master: If a man ever reveals his true self, it is when he is mourning his parents."

19.18. Master Zeng said: "I learned this from the Master: If there is one aspect of Lord Meng Zhuang's filial piety that is beyond imitation, it is the way in which he kept his father's retainers and maintained his father's policies."

19.19. The Meng Family appointed Yang Fu as judge. Yang Fu asked advice from Master Zeng. Master Zeng said: "The authorities have lost the Way; the people have been without guidance for too long. Whenever you solve a case, do it with compassion, and not with a feeling of victory."

19.20. Zigong said: "Zhouxin was not as evil as his reputation. This is why a gentleman hates to dwell downstream of public opinion: all the filth of the world drifts there."

19.21. Zigong said: "A gentleman's mistake is like an eclipse of the sun or the moon. He makes a mistake, and everyone takes notice; he corrects his mistake and everyone looks up in admiration."

19.22. Gongsun Chao of Wei asked Zigong: "From whom did Confucius derive his learning?" Zigong said: "The Way of King Wen and King Wu never fell into oblivion, it always remained alive among the people. The wise retained its essentials, the ignorant retained a few details. All of them had some elements of the Way of King Wen and King Wu. There is no one from whom our Master could not have learned something; and there is no one who could have been our Master's exclusive teacher."

19.23. Shusun Wushu was conversing at court with some ministers and said: "Zigong is better than Confucius." Zifu Jingbo told this to Zigong. Zigong said: "It is like a surrounding wall: the height of my wall only reaches to the shoulder; at one glance, any passerby can see the beauty of the building inside. Our Master's wall is many times taller than a man's height; unless you are allowed in through the gate, you cannot imagine the splendor and wealth of the ancestral temple and the hundred apartments inside. But few are those who are granted access! Your master's observation is therefore not so surprising."

19.24. Shusun Wushu slandered Confucius. Zigong said: "It does not matter. It cannot touch him. The merits of other people are like a hill across which you can walk; but Confucius is like the sun or the moon, over which you cannot jump. If someone wished to cut himself off from their light, how could this affect the sun and the moon? He would merely display his own folly."

19.25. Chen Ziqin said to Zigong: "Sir, you are too modest; in what respect could Confucius be considered your superior?"

Zigong said: "With one word, a gentleman reveals his wisdom; with one word, he betrays his ignorance—and that is why he weighs his words carefully. The Master's achievements cannot be equaled, just as the sky cannot be scaled with a ladder. Had the Master been entrusted with the running of a country or of an estate, he would have accomplished the saying: 'He raised them, and they stood up; he led them, and they marched; he offered them peace, and they flocked to him; he mobilized them, and they echoed his call; in life, he was glorified; in death, he was mourned.' How could his achievements ever be equaled?"

Chapter 20

20.1.   Yao said:

>   Oh, Shun!
> The Heavenly succession was bestowed upon you;
> Hold faithfully the Middle Way!
> Should the people within the Four Seas fall into distress
>   and penury
> This Heavenly gift will be withdrawn forever.

Shun passed this message to Yu.

Tang said: I, the little one, dare to sacrifice a black bull, and dare to proclaim this to the most august sovereign God: I dare not forgive those who are guilty; your servants cannot hide anything from you; you have already judged them in your heart. If I am guilty, do not punish the people of the ten thousand fiefs on my account; if the people of the ten thousand fiefs are guilty, let the fault be on my head.

Zhou enfeoffed many vassals. Good people prospered.

>   Although I have my own kinsmen, I prefer to rely upon
>   virtuous men.

>   If the people do wrong, let their fault be on my head.

Set standards for weights and measures, re-establish the offices that have been abolished, and the authority of the government will reach everywhere. Restore the states that have been destroyed; revive interrupted dynastic lines, reinstate political exiles, and you will win the hearts of the people all over the world.

Issues that matter: people; food; mourning; sacrifice.

Generosity wins the masses. Good faith inspires the trust of the people. Industriousness ensures success. Justice brings joy.

20.2. Zizhang asked Confucius: "How does one qualify to govern?" The Master said: "He who cultivates the five treasures and eschews the four evils is fit to govern." Zizhang said: "What are the five treasures?" The Master said: "A gentleman is generous without having to spend; he makes people work without making them groan; he has ambition but no rapacity; he has authority but no arrogance; he is stern but not fierce." Zizhang said: "How can one be 'generous without having to spend'?" The Master said: "If you let the people pursue what is beneficial for them, aren't you being generous without having to spend? If you make people work only on tasks that are reasonable, who will groan? If your ambition is humanity, and if you accomplish humanity, what room is there left for rapacity? A gentleman treats equally the many and the few, the humble and the great, he gives the same attention to all: has he not authority without arrogance? A gentleman dresses correctly, his gaze is straight, people look at him with awe: is he not stern without being fierce?"

Zizhang said: "What are the four evils?" The Master said: "Terror, which rests on ignorance and murder. Tyranny, which demands results without proper warning. Extortion,

which is conducted through contradictory orders. Bureaucracy, which begrudges people their rightful entitlements."

20.3. Confucius said: "He who does not understand fate is
incapable of behaving as a gentleman. He who does not understand the rites is incapable of taking his stand. He who does
not understand words is incapable of understanding men."

NOTES

1.1. *the right time:* or "the prescribed time" (this meaning is found in Mencius). Zhu Xi's interpretation, "all the time," "constantly," is an anachronism—reading an ancient expression in the misleading light of a later usage.

gentleman: before Confucius, the word *junzi* (gentleman) merely indicated social status. A major originality of Confucian thought is to have progressively divested this notion of its social definition and to have endowed it with a new, purely ethical content. This transformation had huge and radical implications, as it was eventually to call into question the fundamental structure of the aristocratic-feudal order. For the old concept of an hereditary elite it substituted the notion of an elite based not upon birth or wealth, but purely determined by virtue, culture, talent, competence, and merit. Naturally such a transformation did not take place all at once; throughout the *Analects,* one can identify various stages of the concept: in a very few places, *junzi* is still used in its original, narrowly social meaning; more often, it is found in an ambiguous sense which confuses social rank and moral quality. The originality of the Confucian view is fully displayed in the many occurrences where it is the moral dimension of *junzi* which is exclusively developed: on ethical grounds, a commoner can achieve the quality of "gentleman," whereas an aristocrat can lose his qualification for such a title.

Pondering over the evolution of words in Western culture, C. S. Lewis made some observations which could also be apposite here:

> Words which originally referred to a person's rank—to legal, social or economic status and the qualifications of birth which have often been attached to these—have a tendency to become words which assign a type of character and behaviour. Those implying superior status can become terms of praise; those implying inferior status, terms of disapproval. *Chivalrous, courteous, frank, generous, gentle, liberal,* and *noble* are examples of the first; *ignoble, villain,* and *vulgar,* of the second. . . .
>
> It will be diagnosed by many as a symptom of the inveterate snobbery of the human race; and certainly, the implications of language are hardly ever egalitarian. But that is not the whole story: Two other factors come in. One is optimism; men's belief, or at least hope, that their social betters will be personally better as well. The other is far more important. A word like *nobility* begins to take on its social-ethical meaning when it refers not simply to a man's status but to the manners and character which are thought to be appropriate to that status. But the mind cannot long consider those manners and that character without being forced on the reflection that they are sometimes lacking in those who are noble by status and sometimes present in those who are not. Thus from the very first the social-ethical meaning, merely by existing, is bound to separate itself from the status-meaning. Accordingly, from Boethius down, it becomes a commonplace of European literature that the true nobility is within, that *villanie,* not status, makes the villain, that there are "ungentle gentles" and that "gentle is as gentle does." The linguistic phenomenon we are considering is therefore quite as much an escape from, as an assertion of, that pride above and servility below which, in my opinion should be called snobbery. The behaviour ideally, or

optimistically, attributed to an aristocracy provides a paradigm. It becomes obvious that, as regards many aristocrats, this is an unrealised ideal. But the paradigm remains; anyone, even the bad aristocrat himself, may attempt to conform to it. A new ethical idea has come into power.

I think its power has been greatest at the frontier where the aristocrats and the middle-class meet. The court takes from the class below it talented individuals—like Chaucer, say—as its entertainers and assistants.... By expecting to find realised at court the paradigm of courtesy and nobility, by writing his poetry on the assumption that it was realised, such a man offers a critique of the court's actual *ethos*, which no one can resent.... As they say a woman becomes more beautiful when she is loved, a nobility by status will become more "noble" under such treatment. Thus the Horaces, Chaucers, Racines, or Spensers substantially ennoble their patrons. But also, through them, many graces pass down from the aristocracy into the middle class. This two-way traffic generates a culture-group comprising the choicest members of two groups that differ in status. If this is snobbery, we must reckon snobbery among the greatest nurseries of civilisation. Without it, would there ever have been anything but wealth and power above and sycophancy or envy below? (C. S. Lewis, *Studies in Words* [Cambridge, 1967], 21–23)

C. S. Lewis's final observations on the crucial role played by the culture group at the frontier where aristocrats and middle-class meet has particular relevance here, since Confucius and his disciples all belonged to such an intermediate and socially fluid group, the *shi*—on this question, see note 4.9.

1.2. *Master You:* You Ruo, disciple of Confucius. In the *Analects*, only two disciples, You Ruo and Zeng Shen (who appears in 1.4) are *consistently* given the title of Master. For this reason, several commentators have concluded that the *Analects* were probably compiled by disciples of these two disciples.

A man who respects his parents and his elders would hardly be inclined to defy his superiors: filial piety at home is a guarantee of docility in public life—dutiful sons are unlikely to become rebellious subjects. "State Confucianism" (the imperial manipulation of Confucian thought for political purposes, which was eventually to give such a bad name to Confucianism in modern times) focused on passages such as this and extolled them out of context. Although filial piety is indeed a very important precept, one cannot reduce the ethics and politics of Confucius to this sole notion without committing a gross distortion.

humanity: to be understood either in the meaning *man(kind),* or in the meaning *humaneness* (the supreme Confucian virtue, see note 4.1). In Chinese, the two words are homophonous *(ren)* and their graphic structure is closely related. Which reading should be adopted here? Commentators hesitate.

1.3. *goodness:* or, more literally, "humanity" *(ren)*—the supreme Confucian value, just mentioned above, and more fully discussed in note 4.1.

1.4. *I examine myself three times a day:* a majority of Western translators write: "I examine myself every day on three points." Chinese commentators generally reject such a reading, for syntactic reasons (the "Western" interpretation would require, instead of the original phrase *wu ri san xing,* the construction *wu ri xingzhe san*—on the same pattern as that in 14.28: *junzi daozhe san.*) The fact that the examination actually bears on three points is a mere coincidence.

1.5. *a state of middle size:* literally, "a state of a thousand chariots"—*sheng,* a war chariot drawn by four horses. The importance and power of a country were measured by the number of war chariots it could align on the battlefield. At the beginning of the Spring and Autumn period (700 B.C.), even the biggest states could not muster a thousand chariots—for instance, at the battle of Chengpu, Duke Wen of Jin had only seven hundred chariots (*Zuo Zhuan*, 28th year of Duke Xi). Later on, however, with the increasing incidence of warfare, the various states developed their armaments; at the time of the Pingqiu Conference (*Zuo Zhuan*, 13th year of Duke Zhao), Jin could put four thousand chariots in the field. In the time of Confucius, a state of a thousand chariots was no longer a major power; see for instance Zilu's statement (11.26): "Give me a state of a thousand chariots, hard pressed by powerful neighbors . . ."

mobilize the people only at the right times: so as not to interfere with the seasonal tasks of agriculture.

1.6. *study literature:* purely intellectual and cultural activities should be pursued only in leisure time. All learning is first and foremost for the purpose of moral improvement, whereas the acquisition of mere knowledge is of secondary importance. The highest achievement of education is righteous behavior (see for instance 1.14).

1.7. *Zixia:* courtesy name of Bu Shang; disciple of Confucius. As it was offensive to call a man by his personal name (which implied control over him; compare with the Biblical taboo forbidding the spelling of the name of God!), in Chinese traditional society everyone had a courtesy name, which could be freely used in social contacts.

A man who values virtue more than good looks: one could also translate, more literally, "who values virtue and *spurns sex (yi se)*." A modern commentator, Yang Bojun, has observed that the rest of the passage refers to three other basic human relations (parents, sovereign, friends) and therefore believes that the first sentence might concern the conjugal link; if this is the case, one might translate "a man who values the virtue (of his wife) rather than her beauty." Note that *yi se* can lend itself to various other interpretations: "to modify one's attitude" (in order to express respect to virtuous people)," or simply, "to control one's countenance (or expression)."

1.8.   *his learning will remain shallow:* literally, "his learning will not be solid." Two other interpretations are also possible: "if he studies, he will not remain inflexible"; or, "if he studies, he will not remain uncouth." It all depends in which acceptation we understand the word *gu:* all three senses (solid, inflexible, uncouth) are found in different passages of the *Analects.*

1.9.   *When the dead are honored and the memory of remote ancestors is kept alive, a people's virtue is at its fullest:* on this very important subject, see note 10.25.

1.10.   *Ziqin:* courtesy name of Chen Gang, whom we shall meet two more times later on (16.13 and 19.25). He does not seem to have been a disciple of Confucius, though the opinion of commentators is not unanimous on this point.

Zigong: courtesy name of Duanmu Si; disciple of Confucius.

1.12.   *practicing the ritual:* the rites represent a fundamental Confucian value, more or less equivalent to our concept of "civilization." On the formal level, they constitute a sort of liturgy, but like our own liturgical rites, these forms, when properly understood and performed, are not hollow: they are efficient and operative, they regulate and teach. When the ritual practice becomes loose, civilization is eroded and barbarism creeps in. (See also note 12.1.)

harmony cannot be sought for its own sake: one is reminded of St Augustine (*Confessions,* X, 33) who developed ambivalent feelings regarding the beauty of Church music. In the end, he suspected that what touched him most was the song rather than what was sung, and that this could become a sinful indulgence.

1.13. *The best support ...:* this whole sentence is obscure; the original text is probably corrupt. Commentators and translators have twisted and tortured these few enigmatic words in the hope of pressing a few drops of meaning out of them. Among modern Chinese commentators, the most reliable guides generally agree to interpret *yin* and *zong* in the sense "to rely upon," "to follow." Others believe that *yin* might stand for another character with the same pronounciation, meaning "to marry"; they interpret the sentence as a precept regarding the choice of a "suitable bride" *(ke qin),* worthy to be introduced to the "ancestors" *(zong).* There are still other interpretations, all of them most ingenious and imaginative. I prefer not to join the competition.

It must have been this sort of debate that inspired J. L. Borges's comment:

> Around 1916, I decided to apply myself to the study of Oriental literatures. As I was reading with credulous enthusiasm the English translation of a certain Chinese philosopher, I came across this memorable passage: 'It matters little to a convict under a death sentence if he has to walk on the edge of a precipice; he has already given up living.' To that phrase, the translator had appended an asterisk, and indicated that his interpretation was to be preferred to that of a rival sinologist who had translated 'The servants destroy the works of art so as not to have to adjudicate on their merits and defects.' At that point, like Paolo and Francesca, I did not read any further. A mysterious skepticism had crept into my soul. (*Œuvres complètes* [Paris: Gallimard-Pléiade, 1993], vol. 1, 1183. My translation.)

1.15.   *Poems:* the *Book of Poems* is an anthology allegedly compiled by Confucius; it comprises folk songs and ceremonial hymns (on its use and interpretation, see note 2.2.)

Zigong's quote refers to Poem 55 (Mao edition, used here for all further references), which describes a nobleman's dignified bearing. The moral lesson to be drawn from these lines was that a gentleman must constantly control and improve his character.

2.2. *Think no evil: Book of Poems,* Poem 297. In their original context, these three words *(si wu xie)* merely describe a chariot being drawn on a straight course, and *si* does not mean "to think"—it is simply an auxiliary particle. Confucius manipulates the *Book of Poems,* quoting lines out of context and producing deliberate misunderstandings in a way which reflects a perfectly legitimate and accepted practice of his time. In formal circumstances, etiquette required statesmen, diplomats, and gentlemen not to express themselves in their own words; instead, they had to borrow the authority of canonical books, and their speech was a patchwork of phrases lifted out of the scriptures, in a way somehow reminiscent of Huxley's character in *Brave New World,* who talked exclusively in Shakespearean quotations—or again, like those who compose anonymous letters by cutting words or phrases out of books or newspapers, and pasting them together on a piece of paper. The *Book of Poems* was the richest and most handy repository of such materials. Whether it was Confucius himself, as a tradition maintains, who actually edited the anthology of three hundred pieces that we still know today, cannot be ascertained; but the fact remains that the *Book of Poems* occupied a central place in the education which he gave to his disciples. Without an ability to recite the *Poems* and to quote from them with utter versatility, no man could be deemed educated, nor would he have had any means to express himself in ceremonial functions.

2.3. *cunning ... a sense of participation:* I am transposing rather freely two words which, in this particular context, seem to mean respectively "to stay out of trouble" *(mian)* and "to submit willingly" *(ge).*

2.4. *my ear was attuned:* the original text is obscure and perhaps corrupt. Endless comments and theories have been propounded in various attempts to explain the two words *er shun.* None seems fully convincing.

At seventy, I follow all the desires ...: although the Chinese language has no tenses, my translation shifts here to the present. Since Confucius died in his early seventies, at this particular point he must have been describing his present condition.

2.5. *Meng Yi:* belonged to one of the great families of the dukedom of Lu.

Fan Chi: disciple of Confucius.

2.6. *Meng Wu:* son of Meng Yi.

2.7. *Ziyou:* courtesy name of Yan Yan, disciple of Confucius.

2.8. *It is the attitude that matters:* literally, "what is difficult is the expression"—which can be understood in two different ways: either that the dutiful son must manage a kind and respectful expression when he attends to his parents' needs; or that he must be capable of interpreting his parents' expression in order to guess whether they are pleased with his services.

Note that Confucius has just given *four* different answers to one and the same question. This is a characteristic feature of his pedagogy: he does not teach abstract notions, he always adjusts his teaching to the concrete needs and specific personality of the person whom he is addressing. Later on, we shall encounter even more striking examples of this principle: one should not teach the same thing to different people.

C. G. Jung wrote to a correspondent: "Not everybody needs to know the same thing, and the same knowledge should never be imparted to all in the same way. This is what is utterly lacking in our modern universities: the relation between master and disciple." And, as it was suggested to him that he should establish an institute of comparative research into Eastern and Western thought, he replied "For me an institute that dispenses wisdom is an utter abomination. As far as I know, neither Confucius nor Zhuang Zi ever ran an institute." (C. G. Jung: *Correspondance*, vol. 1, 1906–1930 [Paris: Albin Michel, 1992].)

2.9. *Yan Hui:* Confucius's favorite disciple. His courtesy name was Ziyuan.

2.12. *a pot:* one might also translate "a utensil" or "a tool"— the idea is the same: the capacity of a gentleman is not limited as is that of a container; his abilities are not circumscribed to one narrow and specific function, like a tool which is designed for only one particular purpose. The universal aim of Confucian humanism should have particular relevance for us today, as our modern universities seem increasingly concerned with the mere training of "specialized brutes."

The civil service which was to run China with great efficiency for two thousand years embodied the Confucian ideal: officials were selected through an examination system that essentially tested their knowledge of the Classics and their literary talent. With such an intellectual equipment, a local prefect was expected to dispatch single-handedly all the affairs

of a large territory with a vast population, performing simultaneously the functions of administrator, judge, engineer,
economist, police officer, agronomist, architect, military commander, etc. (not to mention that, in his leisure time, he was
also supposed to be a competent calligrapher, poet, writer,
painter, musician, and aesthete).

Regarding the syntax of this passage, S. W. Durrant ("On
translating *Lun Yü,*" in *Chinese Literature: Essays, Articles;
Reviews,* January 1981, vol. 3) objected to the type of translation which I am adopting here, saying that it treats the preverbal negative particle *bu* as if it were the pre-nominal negative particle *fei.* This objection is pertinent only in appearance:
it ignores the morphological fluidity of the Chinese language.
One can account for the negative *bu* by treating "pot" as a
verb: "a gentleman does not act-as-a-pot" or "does not *pot-
ify*"—if such a neologism could be forgiven.

Finally, it should be observed that, if we were to take *qi* in
the sense of "utensil," "tool," the passage could also be translated "A gentleman does not let himself be manipulated."

2.16. *To attack a question from the wrong end ...:* here, the
original text is not corrupt, and yet its interpretation poses
intriguing problems: the passage can be read in various ways,
sometimes eventuating in opposite meanings! It all depends
how the syntax is tackled, and what sense is ascribed to three
words—*gong, yiduan,* and *yi.*

The most common interpretation is: "to apply oneself to the
study of heterodox doctrines, this is harmful indeed." *Gong*
has two possible meanings: "to attack" and "to study." Was
the latter sense already in use at the time of the *Analects?*
Besides this passage, *gong* is found in three other places in
the *Analects*—each time with the meaning "to attack." *Yiduan*
literally means "the other end"; it came eventually to mean

"heterodox doctrine," "heresy." If one considers that there was no Confucianism in the time of Confucius, and therefore little possibility for heresy, an alternative interpretation can be suggested: "erroneous doctrine." This however leaves a grammatical problem unresolved: why is the direct object "doctrine" linked to the verb *(gong)* with a preposition *(hu)?*

Qian Mu proposed an ingenious solution, keeping *gong* in its original sense "to attack," "to oppose," and *yiduan* in its concrete meaning "the other end"—therefore also: "the other side," "the other party," "the contradictor." In English, one could paraphrase his reading as: "to persist relentlessly in refuting contradictors, this is harmful indeed." Yet, is this beautiful interpretation (which is grammatically unimpeachable) not ideologically biased, reflecting the Confucian faith of a great traditional scholar? Is Qian Mu not determined at all costs to present Confucius as an enlightened advocate of tolerance? In the other camp, Yang Bojun, a scholar from the People's Republic, who is not encumbered with theological preconceptions and looks at the *Analects* from the dispassionate angle of a linguist, a grammarian, and a social historian, proposes a radically new interpretation for this passage: "attack erroneous doctrines (or, if you like: "smash heresies") and you will put an end to all harms." In this reading, *hai* ("harm") is a noun, subject of *yi,* which functions no more as a final particle, but as a verb, "to stop." This daring interpretation could have disturbing implications for our understanding of Confucius's personality, who would then appear as some sort of fearsome ayatollah!

Still, it leaves two grammatical problems unresolved. The first one has already been mentioned: what should be the function of the preposition *hu?* The second one regards *yi:* this word is indeed found elsewhere in the *Analects,* as a verb meaning "to stop"; what we have here, however, is not *yi* alone, but the compound expression *yeyi*, which, in the *Analects*, is always used simply to mark the end of a sentence, and possesses no signification of its own.

2.17.   *Zilu:* courtesy name of Zhong You; disciple of Confucius. Active and impetuous, Zilu was a colorful character; among all the disciples, his personality stands out in a way not dissimilar to that of St. Peter in the Gospels.

to take what you do not know for what you do not know, that is knowledge indeed: in one of Victor Hugo's notebooks (posthumously published), there is an observation which offers the corollary of this statement: "There are two ways of ignoring things; the first one is by ignoring them; the second one is by ignoring them while believing that one knows them. The second form of ignorance is worse than the first." Victor Hugo: *Océan* [Paris: Laffont, 1989], 3. (Actually Hugo was merely rephrasing an old principle of navigation: the sailor who does not know his position is less in danger than the one who mistakenly believes that he knows it.

2.18.   *Zizhang:* courtesy name of Zhuansun Shi; disciple of Confucius.

2.19.   *Duke Ai:* ruler of the dukedom of Lu (Confucius's country).

2.20.   *Ji Kang:* belonging to one of the great families of Lu, he was a sort of *maire du palais* and exerted real power in the dukedom.

2.21.   *the Documents:* the passage quoted here by Confucius is not to be found in the *Book of Documents* as it is known today. *The Book of Documents* was a compilation of edicts and admonitions from the early rulers and their wise ministers; it was a fundamental textbook of the Confucian school.

2.22. *yoke-bar ... collar-bar:* more literally, the pin which secures the yoke or the collar-bar to the carriage—i.e., a tiny element on which the very use of the entire contraption depends.

2.23. *If Zhou has successors, we can know what they will be like, even a hundred generations hence:* it might be remarked that, from the time of Confucius to this day, exactly seventy-seven generations have elapsed (if we can trust the genealogical tree of his modern descendant, Kong Decheng, who was born in 1920).

2.24. *gods that are not yours:* one should worship only the gods of one's own land (or the spirits of one's own ancestors). Generally, the compound *guishen* refers to the gods, whereas *gui* (used alone) designates more frequently the spirits of the ancestors; in some instances, however, *gui* can have the broader meaning of the first expression, and—according to Qian Mu and to Yang Bojun—this seems to be the case here. Anyway, the general meaning is clear and fits with all we know of Confucius's position regarding religion: *il faut ce qu'il faut.* That is to say, the requirements of decency, morality, and social order should be met—nothing less, nothing more. With the gods and spirits, one should not overdo things.

3.1. *eight rows of dancers:* only the ruler was entitled to use eight rows (there were eight dancers in each row); the feudal lords could use six rows, and the grand officers, four. The head of the Ji Family belonged to this latter category.

Confucius denounces the way in which members of the aristocratic clans were usurping royal privileges. The ambitions of the great feudal lords were progressively undermining the ancient ritual order, and in its stead the law of the jungle was creeping in. Confucius had a tragic awareness that he was witnessing the disintegration of civilization—and for us today, it is this very awareness that, at times, gives such a modern ring to his anguish.

If he is capable of that: the Chinese phrase here has entered current language use as a proverbial expression, but in this process, it acquired a different meaning: "If we tolerate this, what should we not tolerate." A majority of Western translators have followed this interpretation. However, *ren* ("to tolerate") has in classical Chinese also another meaning: "to dare," "to have the cheek," and both Qian Mu and Yang Bojun prefer to adopt here this second reading. Furthermore, it should be observed that Confucius was not in a position to tolerate or to forbid the impudent usurpations of the Ji clan: he was passing a moral judgment, which he had no power actually to enforce.

3.2. *Yong:* a piece from the *Book of Poems* (Poem 282). As in the previous passage, Confucius attacks a liturgical usurpation that was symbolic of political usurpation.

Here (as for various other passages in this chapter) my translation is not literal: I have supplied a number of words in order to make explicit what was merely implied in the original text.

3.4. *Lin Fang:* commentators merely say that he was from Lu. Aside from his interest in ritual matters, there is no concrete information about him.

3.5. *Barbarians ... are inferior:* this important passage raises fascinating problems of interpretation. There are two ways of reading it—with opposite meanings. It says either "Barbarians who are fortunate enough to have rulers are still inferior to Chinese who do not have such luck," or "Even barbarians have rulers—in this respect, they are unlike (i.e., better than) the Chinese who do not have any."

Through the ages, commentators have inclined now to the first reading, now to the second, in a way that often reflected their own historical circumstances. During the Six Dynasties period, for instance, as China was tragically disunited and half of its territory had fallen to foreign invaders, a majority of commentators followed the first reading; they derived some comfort from the notion that, even in the middle of political chaos, defeated Chinese were still superior to victorious barbarians. It was only by affirming the superiority of their civilization that they managed to define and maintain a cultural identity that was being threatened under foreign occupation.

In the Song period, on the contrary, several commentators

came to prefer the second interpretation. After the traumatic disorders that had marked the end of the Tang and the Five Dynasties, and confronting the permanent threat from northern barbarians which challenged the very survival of the unified empire, the most pressing priority was to maintain a strong central authority that could prevent political disintegration. Therefore, scholars were eager to draw one lesson from the enemy, and for them it became salutary—and urgent—to ponder this paradox: even barbarians can appreciate the advantages of centralized power; are we going to lag behind them in this respect?

The second reading—which allowed a superiority to the barbarians—was naturally bound to please scholars who were not Chinese. Thus Arthur Waley translated without hesitation: "The barbarians . . . have retained their princes. They are not in such a state of decay as we in China". Before him, Fr. Séraphin Couvreur (1895) had already shown the way: "Les barbares qui ont des princes sont moins misérables que les nombreux peuples de la Chine ne reconnaissant plus de princes."

It may be tempting to think that Confucius was able to transcend the limitations of his own cultural world and that he could find some merit in barbarians. Yet would such a reading be justified? It would certainly fit with Confucius's view of the extraordinary importance of the royal authority. The dynastic institutions of Zhou were to him the very cornerstone of civilized order, the only rampart against the ferocious rivalries of the feudal lords. He believed that only a restoration of the king's power could prevent social disintegration. From this point of view, barbarians who kept their kings could quite naturally be extolled as a model for the Chinese to follow.

Yet one could equally develop an opposite reasoning: Confucius did not worship monarchy for its own sake. The king's power was not important in itself—it was valuable only as an instrument and as a condition of civilization. It was *civilization* that constituted the absolute value; civilization alone distinguished the Chinese from the barbarians, and the superiority of the Chinese rested on it: even with their kings, barbarians could not equal civilized nations, though the latter might unfortunately be sometimes deprived of a sovereign.

Still, the final word should belong to philology and not to philosophy. In the end, it all depends on the meaning of *bu ru*—literally, "to be unlike." It seems that in the pre-Qin period (and especially in the *Analects:* see, for instance 5.9 and 6.20), this expression meant nearly always "not to equal," "to be inferior," "not to be as worth." If this is also the case here, we should conclude that Confucius believed that barbarians were inferior to the Chinese. This conclusion is not surprising.

3.6. *Mount Tai:* the Eastern Peak (in Shandong) and the most important of the five holy mountains. To offer a sacrifice to the Spirit of Mount Tai was the exclusive preserve of the Son of Heaven—it was the most solemn and sublime liturgy in the civilized world. The impudence of the head of the Ji Family was downright sacrilegious.

Ran Qiu: Confucius's disciple; his courtesy name was Ziyou (not to be confused with Yan Yan—mentioned in note 2.7.— whose courtesy name Ziyou is written with another character for *you.*) Ran Qiu was in the employment of the Ji clan, and therefore Confucius hoped that he might be able to persuade his master to desist from such an indecent entreprise.

Lin Fang: previously encountered above in the passage 3.4. It is difficult to understand what he is doing here. For some commentators, Lin Fang—who, as we have seen, was interested in ritual matters—may have represented the most basic level of expertise in this field: even a fairly ordinary individual such as Lin Fang had enough knowledge to appreciate the impudence of the head of the Ji clan; if the Spirit of Mount Tai were to approve the latter's sacrifice, he would show even less discernment than Lin Fang. (This explanation seems contrived, but we have nothing better to offer . . .)

3.7. *A gentleman avoids competition:* moral disapproval of competition and of aggressiveness as well as the avoidance of all direct confrontations were to become deeply imprinted upon the Chinese psychology through centuries of Confucian education. This attitude, in turn, was to lead to the modern rejection of Confucianism, which was blamed by revolutionary intellectuals for China's incapacity to fight effectively against Western imperialism. (At the end of the nineteenth century, even a staunch conservative such as Lin Shu—the talented and influential introducer of European literature into China— argued that Chinese society could usefully "learn from the fighting spirit of the Western bandits in order to protect itself against foreign aggression." To this very effect, he translated with huge success no less than eleven novels by H. Rider Haggard—his favorite foreign author. This is how *Joan Haste, She, Ayesha, King Solomon's Mines,* etc. came to have in China a cultural and moral impact which their creator could hardly ever have envisioned.

3.8. *Oh, the dimples . . . :* the first two verses are from the *Book of Poems,* (Poem 57); the third has not been identified.

3.10. *I do not wish to watch the rest:* this sacrifice should have remained an exclusive privilege of the Zhou kings—and yet a mere feudal lord such as the Duke of Lu dared now to perform it, thus provoking the indignation of Confucius, who refused to witness such a scandal.

3.11.   *I do not know:* Confucius not only refuses to attend this sacrifice, which was performed in shocking conditions, but he pretends he understands nothing about it. A world where vassals can usurp the prerogatives of their lord without arousing universal condemnation is a topsy-turvy world. Whoever could clearly perceive this would be in a position to set the world back into order.

3.12.   *Sacrifice implies presence:* in Chinese *ji ru zai* means literally "to sacrifice as if present." The terseness of this statement has given rise to various interpretations—none of which seems fully convincing. Arthur Waley thinks it is a pun; his explanation is very clever—yet the very problem is that his explanations are sometimes too clever by half...

3.13.   *Wangsun Jia:* minister of Duke Ling of Wei—to whose court Confucius had come, seeking employment. The proverbial saying which Wangsun Jia is quoting here is an expression of cynical folk wisdom: rather ingratiate yourself with the servants who can feed you than with their master, whose distant benevolence is of no practical use. The exact intention of Wangsun Jia is not clear. Either he is asking advice for the advancement of his own career: Should he court the favor of the duke ("the god of the house") or of his favorite ("the god of the kitchen")? Or, under the guise of a question, he may be addressing a veiled warning to Confucius: Do not trust the duke too much; if you wish to succeed here, it is with *me* that you will have to deal. The question may be ambiguous, but the answer is clear: Confucius condemns all opportunistic maneuvers—the only right policy is to follow the dictates of morality.

3.15.   *this fellow:* literally, "the son of the man from Zou." (Confucius's father had occupied an official position in the town of Zou.) This form of address was insultingly casual.

3.16. *it does not matter whether one pierces the target:* as it would in the case of a military archer, for instance. A gentleman is content merely to *reach* the target: this is not a contest of strength, but a ritual practice. This conception remained alive in Japan, where ritual archery was eventually to become much admired in our time by naive Western pilgrims in quest of "Oriental mysticism" (see for example Eugen Herrigel's *Zen in the Art of Archery*, which Arthur Koestler cruelly lampooned in *The Lotus and the Robot*).

3.17. *the New Moon Ceremony:* celebrated the handing down of the calendar by the Zhou king to the vassals.

Confucius was witnessing with anguish the terminal erosion of royal authority, as the increasingly savage conflicts between the various lords were threatening the entire civilized order. Confucius took every opportunity to profess his attachment to the Zhou dynasty—which he equated with civilization—and endeavored to preserve at least the symbolic remains of its authority; these were still to be found in various ceremonies, such as this sacrifice which Zigong foolishly wished to simplify.

3.19. *Duke Ding:* of Lu.

3.20. *The Ospreys:* the love song which opens the *Book of Poems* (Poem 1). Note that *yin* (translated here as "lasciviousness") in its original sense meant simply "excess." "Gay without excess" would be a perfectly defensible translation; yet, as Confucius is commenting on a love poem, it seems that the derived meaning (which is more common) should be adopted here.

As to "gay," needless to say, this word is here restored to the rightful meaning it always enjoyed in English before it was paradoxically hijacked by a rather *grim* lobby.

3.21. *Duke Ai:* of Lu.

Zai Yu: Confucius's disciple; his courtesy name was Ziwo.

fir: in the original text it is a chestnut tree *(li)* which enables Zai Yu to make his pun on the people who "fear" *(li)*.

What is done is done . . . : Confucius is highly displeased. What irritates him in his disciple's indiscreet comments is not the fact that he based his argument on a pun (at the time such a method was perfectly acceptable; Chinese ancient thought often favored *analogical* process over *logical* reasoning and, as we shall see, Confucius himself could sometimes indulge in puns which today even Professor Lacan would have found atrocious)—no, the problem is not one of expression, but of content: Confucius blames Zai Yu for justifying political terror and lending it the prestige of ancient tradition.

3.22. *Guan Zhong:* in the seventh century B.C. (roughly a hundred and fifty years before Confucius), he was prime minister of Qi and built up the power and prosperity of his country.

Why is Confucius so harsh on him? The great historian Sima Qian (early first century B.C.) suspected that Confucius's main criticism was that Guan Zhong failed to develop the supreme and sublime ambition of restoring the ancient royal unity of China. He was a skillful politician serving an intelligent lord and running a wealthy and powerful state: he had in his hands all the cards that Confucius was desperately seeking and never succeeded in gathering. Guan Zhong ultimately lacked inspiration and vision, he wasted a unique chance; he could have taken advantage of his situation "to pacify the whole world," but instead he was content merely to ensure the good management of the affairs of Qi.

three palaces: The expression *san gui* is obscure, Various interpretations have been proposed: "three wives," "three residences" . . . One ingenious theory (which was advanced by Guo Songtao) established a connection between this expression and the theoretical writings attributed to Guan Zhong, where it is used to designate a taxation method—one which actually contributed to ensure Guan Zhong's personal wealth. (Guo Songtao [1818–91], an original and interesting mind, is better known in history as the first Chinese diplomat posted in Europe; he was successively the minister of China in London and in Paris [1876–78], and left an intriguing record of his first journey to the West.)

3.23. *What can we know of music . . . :* the entire passage is obscure. Commentators and translators usually breeze through it with much confidence, but the very diversity of their readings seems only to give credit to their imagination. It might be good to remember the wisdom of Jean Paulhan: "In places like this, the best translators are the stupidest: they respect obscurity and do not attempt to understand what the matter is." (Jean Paulhan, *Chroniques de Jean Guérin* [Paris, no date], vol. 2, 126. Paulhan was commenting on a French translation of Lao Zi.)

3.24. *his dismissal:* this misadventure happened repeatedly to Confucius, whose entire career ended in frustration. Although posterity was eventually to worship him as China's "First and Supreme Teacher," it should be remembered that teaching always constituted for him a mere *pis-aller.* His true vocation was politics, and he died with the haunting feeling of having utterly failed in his mission.

3.25. *Hymn of Peaceful Coronation:* literally, *shao* (music); *Hymn of Military Conquest:* literally, *wu* (music). The first piece celebrated the coronation of Shun, the mythical early ruler who attained supreme power through the most civilized process: the wise ruler Yao, having noticed his superior virtue, abdicated in his favor. The second piece celebrated the military victory of King Wu, who destroyed the Shang dynasty and established the rule of Zhou. Although Wu was virtuous, and the last king of Shang was wicked, the latter was nevertheless the legitimate ruler, and the conquest of Wu was originally a rebellion. (This moral dilemma was eventually solved by Mencius, who gave moral justification to tyrannicide: a king who behaves tyrannically is a king no more, and therefore whoever kills him is not a regicide.)

4.1. *humanity: ren*, the supreme virtue, often translated as "goodness," "benevolence," or "virtue." The person who practises it is "the good man," "the virtuous man," "the man fully humane." I have usually translated it "humanity" but occasionally I've used "goodness." (*Ren* is the Pinyin transliteration; the Wade-Giles *jen* is somewhat familiar in English and appears in American unabridged dictionaries, defined as "benevolence toward one's fellow-men" or "a compassionate love for humanity.") Needless to say, all these translations remain irremediably inadequate; the worst misunderstanding would be to paint Confucius in the pale colors of some sort of benign philanthropist or well-meaning social worker. No image could be further removed from the historical reality. For Confucius, *ren*, the plenitude of humaneness, is truly an absolute; it is of inexpressible and blinding splendor; it puts heroic demands upon every individual, and yet remains close at hand in everyday life; no one possesses it, and yet it informs all our endeavors; though it can never be fully grasped, it is constantly revealed in its diverse manifestations. Following a process similar to the transformation of the concept of *junzi* ("gentleman" had implied at first *social* superiority, and then finally suggested *moral* superiority—see note 1.1), *ren* presents a remarkable evolution. Originally, the word had no moral connotation; in archaic usage (still found in the *Book of Poems*) it merely described the virile and manly bearing of a hero. For this primitive acceptation, still pertaining to an epic mentality, was progressively substituted an ethical notion: man considered in his complex moral relationships with others, and in his obligations toward himself. Confucius gave full development to this new moral perception, setting *ren* as the cornerstone of Chinese humanism. (On the origins and transformation of this concept, see Lin Yü-sheng: "The evolution of the pre-Confucian meaning of *jen* and the Confucian concept of moral autonomy," *Monumenta Serica*, vol. 31, 1974–75)

4.3.   *only a good man can hate people:* for Western minds unconsciously imbued with Christian conceptions, this important and provocative idea seems to have been difficult to accept. It is revealing to observe, for example, how Arthur Waley instinctively seeks to twist this passage (arbitrarily telescoping 4.3 into 4.4) and to turn it on its head, so as to neutralize its original pungency: "Of the adage 'Only a Good Man knows how to like people, knows how to dislike them,' the Master said, 'He whose heart is in the smallest degree set upon Goodness will dislike no one.'" In a belabored note, Waley furthermore attempts—unconvincingly—to justify this tampering with the original text.

4.6.   *there may be people who do not have even the small amount of strength it takes but I have never seen any:* this remarkable passage is strangely at odds with the overall tenor of the *Analects*. On the whole, Confucian thought often appears vulnerable to Montherlant's gibe: "The ignoble aspect of most philosophies is that they aim at an optimistic conclusion". The basic Confucian view is that man, if properly taught, will know goodness and, knowing goodness, will put it into practice. This optimistic faith in the irresistible moral power of pedagogy became such an enduring feature of institutional Confucianism that it eventually found its latest and most paradoxical avatar in militant Maoism (the *study* of "Mao Zedong Thought" was seen as the ultimate weapon against all "counter-revolutionary" evils)! In this passage, however, Confucius takes it for granted that man knows goodness and that he has the actual capacity to enact it—the problem is that *he has no real desire to do so.* Confucius reaches here a psychological intuition that there may be a flaw at the very core of man's nature; but he does not seem to have ever pushed this grim exploration any further. (Actually it took another two thousand years before Spinoza would ponder again the puzzling fact that we do not desire what we know to be good.)

4.7.   *one can know your quality:* or "one can know what sort of man you are." According to some commentators, here the character *ren* ("humanity")—Confucius's supreme virtue, translated by "quality"—stands simply for *ren*, "man."

4.8.   *In the morning hear the Way, in the evening die content:* here, I simply reproduce Waley's rendition: I do not see how one could improve upon it.

4.9.   *A scholar:* in Chinese, *shi*. This very important notion is not easy to translate. D. C. Lau evades the problem by putting here "a gentleman" (and thus confusing it with *junzi*). Waley translates it as "a knight," which seems an *antiquated* anachronism, whereas Legge's "scholar" (as well as the *dushu ren* of the modern Chinese commentators) might be called a *modernistic* anachronism. The solution should lie somewhere in between; the French *clerc*, with its medieval connotation, seems a rather good approximation, but there is no exact equivalent in English; *scholar* anticipates a subsequent development of Confucian thought; Confucius set the trend that was eventually to generate the classical figure of the "intellectual" vested with ethical responsibilities and a political mission—but that exemplary character pertains to a later period.

As it should be emphasized once more, Confucius developed his thought in an age of transformation and crisis of Chinese society; his philosophy was both a product and an agent of the cultural metamorphosis that took place in his time. The social fluidity that characterized this period of upheavals was best exemplified in the highly mobile and dynamic class of the *shi*. Originally, the "knights" had constituted the lowest stratum of the aristocracy; from this marginal position, in Confucius's time, they came to form a hybrid class (to which the Master himself and most of his disciples belonged) in search of a new function and a new social definition; their group comprised rejects from the nobility (junior sons without inheritance or position) and up-and-coming commoners equipped only with talent and ambition. After a few hundred years, the *shi*— whom Confucius had provided with an ideology—were eventually to become the ruling elite of the unified empire; recruited and promoted on the basis of their learning and merit, they formed the bureaucracy that was to govern China for the next two thousand years.

4.11.   *a small man:* opposite of the "gentleman," the notion presents a symmetric evolution: it originally had a social meaning (a commoner) for which Confucius substituted a moral content: a mediocre or vulgar person.

4.13.   *showing deference:* literally, "yielding" *(rang)*—a fundamental precept of Confucian political ethics. A gentleman abhors rivalries and eschews conflict and competition; when offered a position of leadership, a decent man should always decline it at first.

4.15. *Shen:* Zeng Shen (Master Zeng) whom we have already met—see 1.4.

reciprocity: shu—according to Confucius's own definition (see 15.24), this virtue consists in "not doing to others what you would not like them to do to you." For some commentators, "loyalty" *(zhong)* would designate here the positive aspect of the same principle. Lengthy glosses have been developed to expound the cardinal importance of *zhong* and *shu*, but they are not very convincing. It is difficult to escape the puzzling feeling that Master Zeng's explanation is rather anticlimactic.

4.20. *the son does not alter his father's ways . . . :* repeats 1.11, in slightly abridged form.

a good son: a son who practices "filial piety" *(xiao)*. Although Confucius repeatedly praised filial piety, it was *imperial* Confucianism which eventually extolled it as its cardinal virtue (let us not forget that Confucius died 350 years before Confucianism became the state ideology!). In later centuries, moral treatises and exemplary tales further developed this theme, pushing it sometimes to distasteful and gruesome extremes—while Confucianism was turned into a doctrine of submissiveness, thus acquiring the oppressive and obscurantist features that made it odious to modern generations and provoked the virulent anti-Confucian movements of the twentieth century. (What these movements completely overlooked, however, was that imperial Confucianism had arbitrarily isolated the precept of obedience, while obliterating the symmetrical duty of *disobedience* that originally complemented it—on this latter aspect, see the following note, 4.26.)

For the Western reader who has never had to bear the tyranny of Chinese tradition, it should be easier to divest the

Analects of the distorting accretions left by two thousand years of authoritarian practice, and to approach Confucius without prejudice. We might then discover in the Confucian views a timely answer to a pressing problem of our own society. On this issue of the communications between old and young, anthropologists are warning us that the breakdown which the modern world is presently witnessing may endanger the very survival of our civilization: "A society which treats its young as a separate entity is going to pay a dreadful price for this shortsighted indulgence: it is a sign that the established generation has lost faith in its own values and is abdicating its responsibility. A society will survive only if it is capable of transmitting its principles and values from one generation to the next. As soon as it feels unable to transmit anything, or when it does not know anymore what should be transmitted, it ceases to be able to maintain itself." (Claude Lévi-Strauss and Didier Eribon, *De près et de loin* [Paris: Jacob, 1988], 221–22. My translation. A complete English translation has been published: *Conversations with Claude Lévi-Strauss* [University of Chicago Press, 1991].)

4.25. *Virtue is not solitary; it always has neighbours:* "virtue" *(de)* or "moral force," or "moral power" (think of the Latin *virtus*) exerts a transforming action; it creates its own environment, radiates influence, and attracts followers. A true king governs simply by *being* "virtuous."

4.26. *pettiness:* in Chinese, *shuo.* The exact meaning of this word is not absolutely clear—some commentators interpret it as "remonstrance," in which case this passage should be read as a warning against the practice of remonstrating with superiors and friends. This would contradict one of the noblest and most heroic aspects of Confucianism: its tradition of bold

speech, political criticism, and moral disobedience. It was a
duty for statesmen and scholars to stand up to the ruler, even
at the risk of their lives, whenever higher principles commanded them to do so. See, for instance, 14.22: "Zilu asked
how to serve a prince. The Master said: 'Tell him the truth
even if it offends him.'"

5.1.   *Gongye Chang:* disciple of Confucius.

5.2.   *Nan Rong:* disciple of Confucius? His identity is uncertain. Commentators often identified Nan Rong with Nangong Kuo, son of Lord Meng Yi, but there is no solid evidence to back this tradition.

5.3.   *Zijian:* courtesy name of Fu Buqi, disciple of Confucius.

5.4.   *a pot:* see note 2.12.

a precious ritual vase: Confucius softens his negative assessment by conceding that, within what is basically an inferior category (narrow professionalism), Zigong still possesses refined talents.

5.5.   *Ran Yong:* disciple of Confucius; his courtesy name was Zhonggong.

good: in Chinese, *ren* (see note 4.1). To convey the full weight of this word, one should paraphrase "someone who has reached the supreme virtue" or "who has achieved the fullness of his humanity," but these unwieldy phrases would impede the free flow of the translation.

5.6.   *Qidiao Kai:* disciple of Confucius; courtesy name: Zikai.

5.7.   *Still, where would we get the timber for our craft?:* I admit
that my reading here is highly unorthodox—only a tiny
minority of commentators would ever consider it. It should be
observed, however, that all the commonly accepted interpretations are contrived and far-fetched, whereas mine at least
sticks to the letter of the text. These other readings pertain
essentially to three types: 1. "Zilu lacks *judgment*" (*cai,* "timber," is then arbitrarily replaced by another character, also
pronounced *cai,* which means "to cut," "to judge.") 2. "Zilu is
impossibly foolhardy—it seems that I never get the right sort
of people" (*cai,* "timber," means also "material," and therefore,
by extension "human material, talent,"—hence; "the right sort
of people"). 3. "Zilu is impossibly foolhardy, and that's not
something worth extolling!" (*cai* is then replaced by another
character *zai,* equivalent of "!").

Quite possibly the text is corrupt and its original meaning
may never be elucidated. Still, it is interesting to observe that
the reason for which the interpretation adopted here was
rejected out of hand by most commentators had nothing to do
with philology—it simply reflected an unconscious and
instinctive prejudice that deserves to be analyzed.

The conventional image of the Chinese scholar (a cliché
popularized for the most part by Ming and Qing theater and
fiction) usually depicted a refined, fragile, and ethereal crea-
ture whose only manual exertions were limited to the handling of delicate writing brushes and paper fans, who lived
among books, contemptuous of all outdoor activities and
averse to rough and violent exercises. In this perspective,
Confucius's adventurous proposal was necessarily seen as a
preposterous joke, which only a character as crazy as Zilu
would ever take in earnest.

Actually, the stereotype that reduced scholars to weakly
figures was not only inaccurate (the very requirements of

their careers in the civil service always obliged Chinese intellectuals to spend a good part of their lives in arduous, long,
and hazardous journeys as they were moved from post to post
across their huge Empire) but also ignored a historical evolution: at least until the Tang period, it was not uncommon for
scholars, writers, poets, and artists to be good horsemen and
swordsmen as well—if not rough drinkers and fighters to
boot. As one goes further back in time, this "epic" side of the
Chinese *persona* appears the more pronounced: in early periods, the practice of sports and a training in martial arts were
a compulsory part of a gentleman's education (in this respect,
it is revealing to note that, in Confucius's time, the Six Arts,
liu yi, which later on came merely to mean the study of the Six
Classics, still comprised *archery* and *charioteering*, put on equal
footing with rites, music, writing, and arithmetic). A history
of the variations of the Chinese sensibility remains to be
written!

Another factor prevented most commentators—and, in
turn, all translators—from ever contemplating that, in this
instance, Confucius might *not* have been talking in jest, and
that is the indifference and ignorance that eventually came to
obliterate all memory of the amazing achievements of early
Chinese navigation and nautical technology. Thus, in the
minds of later readers, the raft which Confucius mentioned
here could only evoke some sort of wretched contraption,
improvised in an emergency, drifting hopelessly out of control, and tossed about at the whim of the waves. What these
readers had forgotten is that nautical engineering had had in
China a long and remarkable history—actually the ships of
the great Western navigators, from Columbus, Magellan, and
Drake down to Cook and Bougainville, were quite primitive
compared with their Chinese forerunners in Song and Ming
times. In fact, before the great square-riggers and clipper

ships of the nineteenth century, and the big iron ships of Laeisz and Erikson, virtually no Western sailing vessel could have competed in size and speed with the earlier Chinese oceangoing junks. These junks themselves had evolved from large rafts—such as the one mentioned here by Confucius— which were plying the high seas, and, according to modern research, may well have succeeded in reaching the American continent many centuries before Confucius's time.

In the fascinating chapter which he devoted to the nautical technology of ancient China, Joseph Needham commented on this very passage:

> Sighing at the recalcitrance of contemporaries to accept his ethical and social teaching, the Master said that he would embark upon a (sailing) raft *(fu)* and visit the Nine Barbarian Peoples in the hope of finding a better audience. The part about the Barbarians was added by later scholiasts, as e.g. in *Shuo Wen*. The great Legge, in his translation, made out that Confucius intended to get on a raft and drift aimlessly at sea. Doubtless he did not know of the existence of excellent sailing rafts, but it was a pity to generate yet one more unnecessarily fatuous occidental conception of China. In fact, the picture of the sage's tall lug-sail breasting the waves of a stormy sea to bring the message of rational social order to men still slaves of superstition has a real sublimity. Well might such a vessel have merited the epithet of "Starry Raft" *(xing cha)* applied long afterwards in Chinese usage to ships of ambassadors. And well might it have voyaged to the Mexic shore. (Joseph Needham, *Science and Civilisation in China* [Cambridge, 1971], vol. 4, pt. 3, 396.)

On the last great seafaring ventures sponsored by the Chinese empire, the expeditions of Zheng He between 1405 and 1433, see Louise Levathes, *When China Ruled the Seas: The*

Treasure Fleet of the Dragon Throne [New York: Simon and Schuster, 1994].

5.8.   *Gongxi Chi:* disciple of Confucius; his courtesy name was Zihua. He was renowned for his expertise in matters of étiquette.

5.9.   *You are not his equal; and neither am I:* literally, "you and I are not his equal": this sentence could also be interpreted: "I agree, he is better than you." It all depends on how one should read the word *yu*—one of the most richly ambiguous words in the language of this period. (Goran Malmqvist, analyzing the text of the *Gongyang zhuan,* identified nine different meanings for this character. See his study "What did the Master say?" in D. T. Roy and T. H. Tsien, eds., *Ancient China: Studies in Civilisation* (Hong Kong, 1978), 137–55. Here, *yu* is either the conjunction "and" ("You *and* I are not his equals"), or it is a verb: to concede, to approve ("*I agree with you,* you are not as good as he"). Grammatically, the first solution (adopted here) appears more likely; nevertheless, the notion that the Master himself could have confessed his inferiority to one of his disciples was unacceptable for many devout Confucianists, who therefore opted for the second reading.

5.11.   *Shen Cheng:* disciple of Confucius? Some commentators think that this may be Shen Dang, whom Sima Qian listed among the disciples in the *Shi ji.*

5.13.   *the nature of things:* in Chinese, *xing,* "nature." A majority of commentators interpret it as *ren xing,* "human nature"—but the problem is that such a reading is in blatant contradiction with what Confucius actually taught. Confucius, it is true, always avoided speaking about *supernatural* matters, but human nature, on the contrary, was for him a constant subject of enquiry, observation, and reflection. It would therefore seem more appropriate to take *xing* in its earlier and more fundamental meaning of *natura rerum*, the essence of reality.

Confucius would certainly have approved of Wittgenstein: *Wovon man nicht sprechen kann, darüber muss man schweigen* ("Whereof one cannot speak, thereof one should remain silent"). A refusal to speak about the unspeakable implies no denial of its existence—on the contrary. Several passages in the *Analects* suggest the powerful mystical drive that inspired the Master and which only silence could adequately convey (see for example 17.19). Words were to be limited to the political, social, psychological, cultural, and historical areas *(wen zhang)*.

5.15.   *Kong-the-Civilized:* Kong Yu, a grand officer from Wei, who was posthumously given the name of "Civilized". It seems that his private behavior had been questionable (according to the *Zuo zhuan*)—and this may explain Zigong's perplexity.

5.16.   *Zichan:* courtesy name of Gongsun Qiao, grandson of Duke Mu of Zheng. He was a brilliant prime minister of Zheng.

5.17.   *Yan Ying:* famous personality (his biography is found in Sima Qian's *Shi ji*), grand officer of Qi.

5.18.   *Zang Sunchen:* grand officer of Lu. Confucius either blames him for his lack of wisdom (in earlier periods tortoises had been associated with divination; in providing his pet tortoises with lavish accommodation, Zang was yielding to superstition) or he reproaches him for his most impertinent usurpation of a royal privilege (only the sovereign could keep tortoises in such a ritual setting).

5.19.   *Ziwen:* courtesy name of Dougou Wutu.

Cui Zhu and *Chen Xuwu* were both grand officers of Qi.

5.20.   *Lord Ji Wen:* grand officer of Lu. He was not a contemporary of Confucius, having died shortly before the Master's birth.

5.21.   *Lord Ning Wu:* grand officer of Wei (Wu was his posthumous name).

his stupidity is peerless: in order to survive under despotic rule, one must be able to play the fool. In every period of chaos and tyranny, the Chinese have displayed a superior command of this cynical and subtle art: some of the most brilliant examples were provided by the great eccentrics of the Six Dynasties period, and in our time the Maoist terror provided an occasion to revive this old tradition. For instance, the magazine *Xin Guancha* in its issue of October 1980 reported in detail the experiences of a bourgeois intellectual who managed to live in peace for twenty years by moving to a village, where he successfully made himself pass for an amnesic and illiterate deaf and dumb cripple.

5.22.   *Chen:* the territory of this country covered part of the modern provinces of Henan and Anhui. Confucius stayed there for a while, in the course of his long and adventurous journeys in search of an enlightened sovereign who would give him a chance to put his political ideals into practice. At this stage, Confucius finally begins to realize that he will never be granted such an opportunity; the best he can do now is to return home and train a new generation.

5.23.   *Boyi and Shuqi:* semilegendary figures, famous for their exemplary integrity; they went into self-exile and let themselves starve to death out of loyalty toward their former lord.

5.24. *Weisheng Gao:* commentators believe that he is the same person as the Weisheng who figures in Zhuang Zi and in the *Zhan guo ce* (although *Wei* is written there with another character). Paragon of rectitude, he had made an appointment to meet a girl under a bridge; the girl did not appear and the water began to rise. Obstinately faithful to his promise, Weisheng clung to a pile of the bridge and was drowned by the river in flood.

5.25. *Zuoqiu Ming:* traditionally described as the author of the *Zuo zhuan*, but this tradition has no foundation in fact.

6.1. *the making of a prince:* literally, "Ran Yong could be made to sit facing south"—i.e., could occupy the position of a ruler. Ran Yong was a commoner (on this point, see also note 6.6). The most revolutionary aspect of Confucius's political philosophy was precisely the notion that authority should be devolved not according to birth, but according to individual merit.

6.3. *love of learning:* the main achievements of learning pertain to the *moral* order—not to the intellectual order, which by itself is without value.

6.4. *one measure ... hundred times more:* literally "one *yu*" and "five *bing.*" The exact content of these ancient units of capacity is a highly specialized question into which I frankly prefer not to venture, but I remain quite confident that my translation provides here a fairly adequate approximation of the original meaning.

6.5. *Yuan Xian:* disciple of Confucius; his courtesy name was Zisi.

6.6. *Ran Yong:* because of his modest origin, some questioned whether he was qualified to occupy high political office.

Confucius's view, on the contrary, was that his personal talent was the best qualification.

6.7. *Yan Hui could attach his mind to goodness for three months without interruption:* we already know (6.3) that Yan Hui's extraordinary "love of learning" was reflected in his moral achievements; now we see that his attachment to goodness rested on an exceptional ability of concentrating the mind. In our time, Simone Weil has well analyzed the link between intellectual study and spiritual meditation. She observed that a youth who spends two hours in complete concentration over a geometry problem in his homework can actually be performing a most valid prayer—for the exercise of attention diverts the mind from the selfish ego: "Every time that we really concentrate our attention, we destroy the evil that is in us." And her statement "Attentiveness without an object is prayer in its supreme form" could have been issued by a Zen master. See Simone Weil, "Reflections on the Right Use of School Studies with a View to the Love of God," in *Waiting on God* (London: Routledge and Kegan Paul, 1951), 56.

6.9. *Min Ziqian:* disciple of Confucius; his given name was Sun.

the river Wen: it was the boundary between the countries of Lu and Qi. Min Ziqian was a loyal subject of the Duke of Lu, and therefore did not recognize the authority which the head of the Ji Family had usurped. In Qi, he would be safely out of the latter's reach.

6.10. *Boniu:* courtesy name of Ran Geng, disciple of Confucius. (On the identity of Boniu, see Donald Leslie: "Notes on the Analects," *T'oung Pao*, vol. 49, 1961–62.)

Why does this last meeting take place through a window? Some commentators have advanced subtle ritual explanations.

More simply, was it not fear of contagion? Qian Mu (who referred to a passage from *Huainan zi*) wondered if Boniu's illness was not leprosy.

6.13. *educated man:* in Chinese, *ru;* this word came to mean *Confucian* in later centuries—but what was its meaning in the time of Confucius? It seems that it was a sort of archaic equivalent of our modern concept of "intellectual"; the functions of the *ru* were either political administration or teaching.

6.15. *Meng Zhifan:* this anecdote is also related in the *Zuo Zhuan* (11th year of Duke Ai), but there the character in question is called Meng Zhice.

6.16. *Priest Tuo:* grand officer of Wei country; his courtesy name was Ziyu.

6.21. *average people:* instead of "above average." I am following here the emendation of a modern scholar who believes that, in the phrase *zhong ren yi shang,* the words *yi shang* have been interpolated. (See Mao Zishui: "Lunyu li ji chu yanwen di ceyi" in *Qing Hua xuebao,* II, i, May 1960.)

6.22. *A good man's trials bear fruit:* tentative translation of a rather obscure phrase.

6.23. *The wise find joy on the water, the good find joy in the mountains:* wise and good, mountains and waters are not opposed as mutually exclusive terms; they complete each other in a fecund dialectic coupling—like male and female, active and passive, light and shadow, heaven and earth, fullness and emptiness, etc. For example, where we speak of "landscape," the Chinese speak of *shan-shui,* literally: "mountains-and-water." C. G. Jung much admired Chinese thought for its capacity always "to grasp simultaneously the two opposite poles of every reality"; conversely, he found that "the unilateral character of (Western) thought gives it extra energy, but also condemns it to remain barbarian."

6.25. *A square vase that is not square ... :* this is one of the most terse and enigmatic statements of the *Analects*. Literally: *"Gu* not *gu;* what *gu!* what *gu!"* The *gu* was a certain type of ritual vessel, originally meant to be of square shape, but which eventually evolved as a circular vase. Perhaps Confucius used the example of this paradoxical evolution to illustrate one of his fundamental ideas: the necessity to restore "correct names."

6.26. *Zai Yu asked ... :* this entire passage is quite obscure and my translation is tentative.

6.27. *A gentleman enlarges his learning through literature:* needless to say, the very notion of literature had a very different content in the time of Confucius, but the basic idea that the mind is uniquely enlarged by the literary experience was also expressed in Western culture; see for example this statement by a leading modern critic:

> Literature enlarges our being by admitting us to experiences other than our own ... They may be beautiful, terrible, awe-inspiring, exhilarating, pathetic, comic or merely piquant. Literature gives the entrée to them all. Those of us who have been true readers all our life seldom realize the enormous extension of our being that we owe to authors. We realize it best when we talk with an unliterary friend. He may be full of goodness and good sense but he inhabits a tiny world. In it, we should be suffocated ... My own eyes are not enough for me ... Even the eyes of all humanity are not enough. I regret that the brutes cannot write books. Very gladly would I learn what face things present to a mouse or a bee ...
>
> In reading great literature I become a thousand men and yet

remain myself. Like the night sky in a Greek poem, I see with a thousand eyes, but it is still I who see. Here, as in worship, in love, in moral action, and in knowing, I transcend myself: and am never more myself than when I do. (C. S. Lewis, *An Experiment in Criticism* [Cambridge: Cambridge University Press, 1992], 139–41).

6.28. *Nanzi, the concubine of Duke Ling:* I have supplied the words "the concubine of Duke Ling" to provide the reader with information which every educated Chinese normally possesses. Needless to add that Nanzi did not have a good reputation.

7.1.   *venerable Peng:* various identifications have been suggested, but none is really convincing.

7.2.   *all this comes to me naturally:* this phrase is sometimes interpreted "which of these have I achieved?"

7.3.   *moral power:* in Chinese, *de*—usually translated as "virtue"; this translation would be appropriate if the reader could spontaneously understand it in its original, primary meaning: "virtue," like the Latin "virtus," the Italian "virtù," or the French "vertu," had a connotation of *"power"* which became largely lost in later usage (though striking instances of the old concrete acceptation can occasionally be found in modern literature: for instance, in *Le Rouge et le noir,* Part 2, chap. 19, when, after a painful estrangement, the hero is finally able to climb back into the bed of his new mistress, Stendhal tells us that "La *vertu* de Julien fut égale à son bonheur"—which, in this particular case, means quite literally: "Julien's [sexual] prowess matched his good fortune.")

7.5.   *Duke of Zhou* (twelfth century B.C.): son of King Wen, younger brother of King Wu, uncle of King Cheng, and founding ancestor of Lu, the country of Confucius. The basic institutions of the Zhou dynasty were drafted under his wise counsel. The Duke of Zhou was the great model whom Confucius had dreamed of emulating in his own political career. Now, entering old age, he finally realizes that he will not be afforded the opportunity to achieve a similar enterprise.

7.6. *enjoy the arts:* in Confucius's time, the Six Arts were: rites, music, archery, charioteering, calligraphy, and arithmetic.

7.7. *a token present for his tuition:* literally, "a [small] bundle of [ten slices of] dried meat"—a modest and purely symbolic offering, when students were too poor to afford genuine tuition.

7.11. *whom would you take as your lieutenant?:* Zilu (as we have already had the occasion to note) was more remarkable for his impetuosity than for his good judgment; here he was begging for a compliment: obviously, he expected to be selected as second in command by Generalissimo Confucius. But the latter, who had guessed his ploy, took this opportunity to teach him a sardonic lesson.

7.12. *janitor:* literally, "the official holding the whip." According to the *Record of Rites*, this was a sort of lictor, who opened the way for the king and the feudal lords. The same expression also designated gatekeepers of the market, whose functions were partly those of janitors, and partly those of policemen.

7.14. *the Coronation Hymn of Shun:* literally, *"shao* music"— see *3.25.*

7.15. *Duke of Wei:* Chu, grandson of Duke Ling, and son of a crown prince who had fallen into disgrace. The latter having

come back to claim the throne, the legitimacy of Chu's authority could be questioned, since he was occupying a position that
should normally have belonged to his father.

Boyi and Shuqi: see 5.23. Each of the two brothers being
equally determined to give precedence to the other, they both
refused to succeed to their father's title. In their pursuit of
absolute integrity, they eventually chose to starve to death in
the wilderness rather than compromise with their principles.
Boyi and Shuqi provide an ethical standard: depending upon
one's view of the place which morality should occupy in politics, their fate will appear glorious or deplorable.

In this entire passage, note the art of exploring one issue
under the guise of discussing another one, apparently unre-
lated: Zigong probes Confucius's position on a delicate and
dangerous political problem of pressing actuality, without
mentioning it explicitly—and Confucius manages to indicate
clearly where he stands while talking of something else. Two
thousand five hundred years later, the great political debates
in the People's Republic of China still follow similar methods!

7.17.   *Give me a few more years; if I can study the Changes till
fifty. . . . :* this passage affords various interpretations; the main
alternative reading roughly says: "Give me a few more years:
then, I will have studied for fifty years, and therefore would
become able to avoid any big mistakes." The character *yi,*
which normally designates the title of the *Book of Changes,* is
then replaced by another *yi,* a mere adverb, meaning "also." In
this manner, commentators with rationalist inclinations were
quite happy to get rid of a reference to the *Changes,* which
would otherwise have received here Confucius's most solemn
endorsement. Actually, in spite of its maddening obscurity and
esoteric mysticism the *Book of Changes* remains the most
ancient, most venerable, and most fundamental document in

the entire Chinese culture. It would therefore seem quite natural that Confucius should give it an exceptional importance.

7.18. *dialect ... correct pronunciation:* in everyday life, Confucius spoke dialect. The "correct pronunciation" is the equivalent of the "Mandarin" language of imperial times, or of the National language of contemporary China. This parallel use of dialect in private life and National language in public life persists in China today, even among the ruling elite (and explains in part why so many leading personalities are keen on recruiting their close political entourage among people who come from their own province.)

7.19. *The Governor of She:* literally, "the Duke of She"—Shen Zhuliang, whose courtesy name was Zigao. The territory of She (in today's Henan Province) belonged then to the country of Chu. When the ruler of Chu took for himself the title of King, the Governor of She called himself Duke. This character is mentioned several times in the *Zuo zhuan;* he had a certain reputation for wisdom.

Why did you not say ...: Confucius is proposing here a remarkable and amazing self-portrait. According to the Master, what should define him first and foremost is his joy and enthusiasm as well as a passionate energy that keeps him in a state of spiritual youth: we are far from the tame image of a solemn old preacher, which was eventually to result from centuries of orthodox indoctrination! In complete contrast with the traditional clichés, Confucius's view of himself seems actually much closer to Yeats's "A Prayer for Old Age":

> God guard me from those thoughts men think
> In the mind alone;
> He that sings a lasting song

> Thinks in a marrow bone;
> I pray . . .
> That I may seem, though I die old,
> A foolish passionate man.

7.20. *For my part, I am not endowed with innate knowledge . . . :* in this entire passage, I am essentially following Waley's rendition, which, I think, has just the right inflection.

7.22. *the company of any two people at random:* in Chinese, *san ren xing*—literally: "three people walking," which means: "me and two other people."

7.23. *Huan Tui:* an official in Song country, who attempted to have Confucius murdered. (This episode is briefly recounted in Sima Qian's *Shi ji*).

7.26. *Nothing pretends to be Something, Emptiness pretends to be Fullness, and Penury pretends to be Affluence:* this is Waley's rendition—which seems perfect.

7.27. *The Master fished with a line . . . :* the idea is naturally to give fish and game a fair chance. In an essay published in the twenties, Lin Yutang suggested that the Chinese should learn the Western notion of "fair play"; this proposal provoked in turn a famous and witty rebuttal from Lu Xun, "On Deferring Fair Play." To judge from this passage, it would appear that Confucius was already cultivating fair play some two thousand five hundred years ago.

7.29. *Huxiang:* this place has not been identified.

7.31. *Chen Sibai:* this figure has not been identified. Instead of reading these three characters as the name of a person, some commentators have interpreted them as the title of an official: "the Minister of Justice in Chen country." But it is difficult to see how *sibai* could become an equivalent for "Minister of Justice" *(sikou)*.

Wuma Qi: disciple of Confucius.

Confucius was naturally aware of the fact that Duke Zhao had infringed the ritual taboo that forbade him to marry a woman bearing the same clanic name, but it would have been improper for him to criticize his lord in front of a third party. His final comment ("I am fortunate indeed . . .") is ironic.

In front of a stranger, one should not criticize one's father or one's ruler, however criminal they may be. (Actually, according to the popular axiom, it is not even *conceivable* that a father might be found at fault.) In contemporary China, it was not terror alone that ensured for such a long time the silence of Mao's victims. The persistent influence of Confucian morality acted as a further inhibition.

8.1.   *Taibo:* eldest son of the founding ancestor of the Zhou dynasty. He voluntarily relinquished his position in favor of his younger brother, in order to enable the son of the latter eventually to succeed to the throne (under the name of King Wen), in conformity with the unspoken wish of the Ancestor. To renounce power is the supreme virtue for a statesman— and it is all the more sublime for being performed in greater secrecy.

8.3.   *Look at my feet, look at my hands:* filial piety demanded that a man about to die be able to present in a state of complete integrity the body which he had received at birth from his parents.

Poems: see the *Book of Poems,* Poem 195.

8.4.   *When a bird is about to die, his song is sad; when a man is about to die, his words are true:* "The tongues of dying men / Enforce attention, like deep harmony" (Shakespeare, *Richard II*, 2, 1). In European culture, the myth of the swan song originates with Plato: "For the swans, when they perceive that they must die, having sung all their life long, do then sing more lustily than ever." (*Phaedo*, 85a) The belief that "last words" should be loaded with special wisdom is common to all mankind, even though it seems to run up against obvious physical and psychological obstacles—for dying is usually an absorbing business that leaves precious little time and strength for issuing pithy statements.

Both the need for, and the impossibility of, proferring weighty last words were perhaps best expressed by Pancho Villa. As the Mexican revolutionary lay dying, victim of an assassin (1923), he implored a journalist: "Don't let it end like this. *Tell them I said something.*" (Karl S. Guthke, *Last Words: Variations on a Theme in Cultural History* [Princeton, 1992], 10.)

8.5.   *I had a friend:* traditional commentators believe that this was Yan Hui.

8.9.   *You can make the people follow the Way, you cannot make them understand it:* modern admirers of Confucius have been distressed by the undemocratic character of this statement; they have therefore endeavored to interpret it differently, by modifying its punctuation. (Instead of reading *Min ke shi you zhi, bu ke shi zhi zhi,* they read *Min ke, shi you zhi; bu ke, shi zhi zhi.*) Syntax, however, does not warrant such attempts.

8.10.   *a brave man might rebel:* according to Confucian morality, rebellion is a most heinous crime.

8.18.   *Yu:* the saint who founded the mythical Xia dynasty (third millennium B.C.) (For Shun, see note 3.25)

8.20.   *and yet Shun found only five ministers; as for King Wu:* these words are not in the original; they have been supplied here to make its meaning explicit.

8.21.   *draining floodwaters:* Yu saved his people from a deluge by digging canals and controlling the flow of rivers.

9.1. *The Master seldom spoke . . . :* from other passages in the *Analects,* we know that Confucius avoided two types of topics: those which he found distasteful, and those which are sacred—the unspeakable is either beneath words, or it is beyond words. The trouble with this particular passage is that, here, the two are dealt with jointly: "profit" pertains to the category of the distasteful, whereas "fate" and the supreme virtue of "humanity" belong to the realm of the sacred. (See, for instance, 5.13, where Zigong observes that it is not possible to hear the Master's views on fate—or the "Way of Heaven." Or again, 12.3, where the Master remarks that whoever possesses the virtue of "humanity" is reluctant to speak.) As it seems inconceivable that "profit" should be put on the same footing as "fate" and "humanity," some commentators suggested that the preposition *yu* ("and," "or") should be interpreted here as the verb "to approve of," and one should therefore translate: "The Master seldom spoke of profit; he approved of fate and humanity." Both readings seem equally awkward.

9.2. *With his vast learning, he has still not managed to excel in any particular field:* the man from Daxiang is vulgar indeed, and does not understand that "a gentleman is not a pot" (see

2.12 and its note). Here Confucius pretends ironically that he is going to make up for this alleged shortcoming. Compare with 9.6 and 9.7, where Confucius's manifold skills and specialized competences actually puzzle real gentlemen, and must be excused by the force of circumstances. Confucian education was not an acquisition of technical information, but a development of one's humanity—it was not a matter of *having*, but of *being*. In the universality of his humanism, the Confucian gentleman was the exact equivalent of the *honnête homme* of classical France: see, for instance, Pascal's several reflections on this subject (*Les Pensées de Pascal*, F. Kaplan, ed. [Paris: Cerf, 1982], 543–45. In Brunschwicg edition, nos. 68, 37, 34, 35, and 331; in Lafuma edition, nos. 778, 195, 587, 647, and 533. My translation.):

One does not teach men to be gentlemen, but one teaches them everything else; yet they take pride in being gentlemen, much more than in knowing anything else. The only thing they take pride in knowing is the very thing they never have to learn.

*

It is much more valuable to know something about everything, than to know everything about something. Such universality is the most valuable.

*

In society, you will not acquire the reputation of a connoisseur of poetry unless you adopt the label of a poet, or mathematician, etc. Yet universal minds reject such labels and make hardly any distinction between the crafts of poet and embroiderer. Universal minds are not called poets, or geometricians, etc., but they are all these things, and judges of them too. No one can guess what they are. They will carry on with the conversation on whatever subject happened to be treated when they came in. One does not notice in them that one quality is more conspicuous than another, until it becomes necessary to put it into practice; but then, one remembers that they have such or such an ability, for it is their characteristic that they are not thought of as eloquent unless the question of eloquence is being considered. Therefore it is false praise to say of a man when he comes in, "Here is our expert poet," whereas it is a bad sign for a man if one would not think of submitting some verse to his judgment.

*

Honnête homme: What we should be able to say is not "He is a mathematician" or "a preacher," or "eloquent," but: "He is a gentleman." Such a universal quality alone pleases me. If, as you see a man, you first remember his book, this is a bad sign; I would wish that no particular quality be conspicuous, unless it is called for by the actual circumstance and the opportunity to put it to use *(nothing in excess),* for fear that one particular quality may predominate and generate a label. You should not think of him as eloquent unless eloquence is being required, but then, he should be the very speaker of your choice.

*

We always picture Plato and Aristotle in solemn academic gowns. But they were gentlemen, and as such, used to enjoy a laugh with their friends; and when they amused themselves by composing their *Laws* and *Politics,* they did it for fun: actually it was the least philosophical and serious part of their activity; the most philosophical part was to live simply and quietly. If they wrote about politics, it was as if to lay down rules for a madhouse. And if they pretended to treat it as something very important, it was because they knew that the madmen they were talking to believed themselves to be kings and emperors."

9.3. *The ceremonial cap should be made of hemp:* traditionally, it had to be woven with two thousand four hundred individual threads. To obtain such thin threads from hemp was a very laborious process, whereas silk provided a much more handy material. As this was a purely formalistic requirement, Confucius was willing to adopt the more expedient modern solution. Ritual bowing, however, was meant to convey respect—and on this point, Confucius was not disposed to compromise.

9.5. *The Master was trapped in Kuang:* Kuang was a border town where Confucius nearly fell into the hands of a lynch mob that had mistaken him for Yang Huo, an adventurer who had previously ransacked the region.

9.8. *My mind went blank ... till I worked out something:* I am basically following D. C. Lau's rendition; I agree with his assessment: "the whole section is exceedingly obscure and the translation is tentative."

9.9. *The Phoenix does not come, the River brings forth no chart:* these were the two auspicious omens that announced the coming of a sage and the dawn of an age of universal peace. Confucius believed that Heaven had vested him with a cosmic vocation; in old age, he eventually began to realize that his time was up, and that he would not be given the chance to fulfill the mission for which he had prepared himself all his life.

9.10. *respectfully moved aside:* literally, "he quickened his step" (as a mark of respect), which I have freely transposed into its modern equivalent.

9.13. *a precious piece of jade:* symbol of the sage's talents. Confucius has no intention of keeping his light under a bushel, or of hiding his piece of jade in a box. If he does not pursue a public career, it is not for want of trying. He is still waiting for an enlightened prince who would be able to employ him.

9.14. *to settle among the nine barbarian tribes:* compare with 5.7.

9.15.   *Court pieces ... hymns:* this division appears in the *Book of Poems;* it is difficult to know if Confucius refers here to a poetic or to a musical compilation.

9.17.   *Everything flows like this:* exact equivalent of *panta rhei* (παντα ῥει). Confucius and Heraclitus were contemporaries!

Traditional commentators usually read this passage as an ethical precept rather than as a cosmological statement. Flowing water is a fairly universal metaphor, used not only to suggest constant moral endeavor but also to provide psychological and emotional comfort—see, for instance, Samuel Johnson (*Rasselas,* chap. 35): "Our minds, like our bodies, are in constant flux; something is hourly lost and something acquired ... Do not suffer life to stagnate; it will grow muddy for want of motion: commit yourself again to the current of the world."

9.19.   *It is like the building of a mound ... :* the general meaning is clear enough, but my adaptation is rather free.

9.21.   *I did not see him reach the goal:* because Yan Hui died young. Another meaning is possible: "I never saw him stop." Yan Hui was indefatigable in his love of learning.

9.23.   *How do you know that the next generation will not equal the present one:* it never occurred to the Confucian mind that the next generation might actually *excel* the present one. At the end of the nineteenth century, when the theories of social Darwinism were first introduced to China (thanks essentially to Yan Fu's superb translation of Herbert Spencer's *Evolution and Ethics*), young Chinese intellectuals—and future revolutionaries—were mesmerized. The very concept of "revolution" (which is a Western notion) is predicated upon the belief that the future can be better than the past—which is inconceivable in a Confucian perspective.

9.24.   *How could words of admonition . . . :* this entire passage
is quite obscure; my rendition is tentative and rather free.

9.26.   *one cannot deprive the humblest man of his free will:* Epic-
tetus said the same: "The robber of your free will does not
exist." (Epict., III, 22, 105; quoted by Marcus Aurelius, *Meditations,* XI, 36) Note that, here, it is not merely an elite of
gentlemen that cannot be deprived of their free will *(zhi).* This
irreducible and inalienable privilege of humanity pertains to
all, and even to "the humblest man" *(pifu).* Every individual,
however common or lowly, possesses the full range of the
human potential—he is equipped with all that is required to
make a hero or a saint, equal to the greatest in history: this
notion eventually found its fullest development with Mencius.
(A good modern equivalent of "the humblest man," *pifu,* could
be the concept of "the man in the street" as understood, for
example, by Evelyn Waugh. To a journalist who had said to
him, "You have not much sympathy with the man in the street,
have you," Waugh gave the memorable reply: "You must
understand that the man in the street does not exist. There
are men and women, each one of whom has an individual and
immortal soul, and such beings need to use streets from time
to time.")

9.27.   *Without envy . . . :* quotation from the *Book of Poems,*
Poem 33.

9.31.   *The cherry tree:* this quotation cannot be found in the
Book of Poems as we know it today.
    The moral lesson drawn by Confucius is that the true prob-
lem is not whether the goal is remote, but whether our zeal is
strong.

10.1. *Confucius was unassuming in his manners and spoke with hesitation:* compare with John Henry Newman's precept: "a gentleman is seldom prominent in conversation" (*The Idea of a University*, Discourse VIII, 10). Newman's famous portrait of a gentleman is too long to be quoted here (anyway, many readers will already be familiar with it), but it is intriguing to note its strikingly *Chinese* quality; for Newman, the commanding virtue that should inspire a gentleman's behavior is a "gentleness and *effeminacy* of feeling which is the attendant on civilization." This association between civilization and *femininity* is not so evident in the West, it seems, and would occur more naturally within the context of a philosophical tradition which always ascribed a dominant role to the *yin* principle.

The entire Chapter 10 deals with the proper behavior of a gentleman; it draws from two different sources, which cannot always be clearly distinguished: some of the statements are *descriptive* and refer to what Confucius actually did, whereas other are *prescriptive* and indicate what a gentleman should do. When the subject of the sentence is "Confucius," or when it is "a gentleman," the distinction is obvious; quite often, however, the reader is confronted with an ambiguous "he." On the whole, I have adopted the past tense for the passages that refer to Confucius, and the present tense for those that concern the model gentleman; but in some instances, the distinction is somewhat arbitrary.

10.5. *holding the jade tablet:* this passage refers probably to the execution of diplomatic missions abroad.

10.6. *purple or mauve lapels:* these two colors were to be avoided, for they are close to black, which was exclusively reserved for ritual and official purposes.

red and violet: too luxurious for daily wear at home.

lambskin, deerskin, fox fur: respectively black, white, and yellow—to match the color of the robe.

shorter right sleeve: for the convenience of manual activities?

nightgown of knee length: most commentators and translators have opted for a literal reading: "half as long again as a man's height." As this would be a ludicrous length for a nightgown, some commentators have suggested that the passage referred in fact to the bed cover. Qian Mu, however, pointed out that *shen* (referring to body size) had two different meanings: 1. the length from the head to the feet; 2. the length from the head to the waist. If one takes the word in the second acceptation, "one *shen* and half" would roughly amount to a length reaching down to the knees—which seems indeed a sensible length for a gentleman's nightgown.

apart from his ceremonial robe, which is of one piece, all his clothes are cut and sewn: the words *which is of one piece* and *and sewn* are not in the original; I have supplied them to make the meaning explicit.

lambskin and black caps: black was always considered absolutely unsuitable for mourning.

10.8.   *he does not gorge himself:* another reading of the character *yan* is possible: "He has no objection to his rice being of the finest quality, nor to his meat being finely minced."

if it is not served at the right time: the expression is ambiguous and can mean either that the food should be served at the right moment of the day or that it should be appropriate for the season.

10.14.   *the eastern stand:* place of honor.

10.16.   *I dare not taste it:* Arthur Waley comments: "A *chün-tzu* (gentleman) takes no medicine except that administered to him by a doctor whose father and grandfather have served the family. Compare the attachment of the English *chün-tzu* to the 'old family doctor.' "

10.17.   *He did not inquire about the horses:* splendid manifestation of Confucian humanism! To appreciate it fully, one should remember that, in Confucius's time, a horse was much more valuable than a stable hand.

A late Chinese commentator attempted to punctuate this passage differently (instead of *"Shang ren hu?" Bu wen ma,* he read: *"Shang ren hu bu?" Wen ma*). It would then mean: "He asked: 'Was anyone hurt?' and then inquired about the horses." The suggestion of this particular commentator was that the Sage's concern extended to all creatures: therefore, in proper order, he first inquired about the people, and then about the horses. That Confucius should also have shown concern for the fate of some horses would probably evoke sympathetic echoes in the West, where many illustrious exponents of a similar attitude are to be found, from Saint Francis of Assisi down to the British Queen Elizabeth II—unfortunately, this reading has no sound philological foundation; it rests upon a gross grammatical anachronism, and was never invoked, except as an amusing illustration of the sort of ambiguities that can result from the absence of punctuation in classical Chinese.

10.21.   *When visiting the grand temple:* with a slight modification, this sentence repeats the opening of 3.15.

10.22.   *A friend died:* respect for the dead is of fundamental importance in Confucian ethics; see note 10.25.

10.23.   *sacrificial meat:* to be used for the ancestors cult; see note 10.25.

10.25.   *ceremonial cap:* Qian Mu suggests that, instead of the character *mian* ("ceremonial cap"), one should read here the character *wen* ("mourning dress"). It would certainly tally with the context.

Respect for the dead is an obligation of such momentous significance that it even entails respecting those who respect the dead—hence, Confucius's reverent attitude toward all people in mourning, however lowly their condition. As Ernst Jünger observed: "Culture is based on the treatment of the dead; culture vanishes with the decay of graves." This notion was always at the heart of every humanistic civilization; now, however, the values for which Antigone was willing to give her life in the classical age of our culture seem to have become only a dim memory in the modern consciousness, and the manifestations of piety toward the dead, which are to be found in all the classics—be they Chinese or Greek—will probably require explanatory notes for future readers.

Raymond Carver, perhaps one of the most sensitive witnesses of our present cultural collapse, has given a chilling illustration of this deterioration in one of his stories, "So Much Water So Close to Home." On an outing, three friends accidentally come across the naked body of a murdered woman;

as they do not want to spoil a fishing weekend in the woods, they wait another two days before reporting their discovery. On learning this, the wife of one of the fishermen feels an irrepressible urge—which she cannot explain—to attend the funeral of the unknown victim.

peddler: I am following Qian Mu's interpretation (*fan* instead of *ban*). The usual rendering "a person carrying official documents" seems much less plausible.

a sudden clap of thunder or a violent gale: these are heavenly omens.

10.27.   *Startled, the bird rose up . . . :* the obscurity of this entire passage has acted as a dangerous stimulant upon the imaginations of many commentators. It seems in fact that the original text has become hopelessly garbled and corrupt; there would be little point in insisting on making sense out of it.

11.1. *Before taking office:* these words are not in the original text; I supplied them to make the meaning explicit.

noblemen: literally *junzi,* "gentlemen"; this is one of the few instances in the *Analects* where the word "gentleman" is used in its original, narrow social acceptation (gentleman *by birth,* aristocrat), as opposed to the new Confucian concept of the moral man.

One of the most progressive aspects of Confucianism as a sociopolitical doctrine was its emphasis upon universal education. As Bernard Knox has observed (in the context of Classical Greece), education is democratic by its very nature: "In a closed aristocratic society, you would not have too much need for education: aristocratic minds tend to think alike. The young aristocrat did not need rhetoric and eloquence to win a place in society; it was already won ... The aristocrat knows by instinct—by blood, he would say—the duties and privileges of his caste. It is characteristic of an aristocracy in fact to find education rather suspect; a man who has to learn the way things are done is by definition an outsider." (*The Oldest Dead White European Males and Other Reflections on the Classics* [New York: Norton, 1993], 88). (Some years ago, the Prince of Wales, being asked by a journalist how he was preparing himself for his future role as British monarch, replied: "I am learning like monkeys do: simply by watching my parents." This is a typically *aristocratic* remark.)

11.2. *none is still with me:* this saying is obscure and has been interpreted in diverse ways. Is Confucius complaining about the ingratitude of earlier disciples who abandoned him? But there is no historical evidence to support such a reading. Or is Confucius merely lamenting the passing of time—one entire generation of disciples has already left? Some commentators try to link this passage with *Mencius*, VII, 2, 18, and think that Confucius is retrospectively attributing his troubles in Chen to the fact that, at the time, he had no connections within the local court; in order to reach such a meaning here, however, one must twist artificially the words of this passage. The same objection also applies to another interpretation: "none obtained official appointment."

11.3. *Virtue: Yan Hui . . . :* some commentators believe that this is a continuation of 11.2: as Confucius had just evoked the disciples who had followed him in Chen and Cai, he then continued with a comment on their respective achievements: "Among those who showed virtue, there was Yan Hui, etc." This interpretation runs up against two difficulties: 1. not all of the ten disciples mentioned here had followed Confucius to Chen; 2. the statement cannot be put in the mouth of Confucius, who always used the familiar form of address when mentioning his disciples, or when talking to them. Here, they are all designated in formal fashion, by their courtesy names, and not by their personal names. This passage must be a comment from the early compilers of the *Analects*, who attempted to summarize, under four headings, the main talents of ten disciples.

11.6. *A flaw in a white jade scepter . . . :* this is the full quotation, whereas the *Analects* quoted only two words. These lines come from the *Book of Poems* (Poem 256). Nangong Kuo, if we accept his identification with Nan Rong (see 5.2), was remarkable for his circumspection.

11.11. *I was not given the chance to treat him as my son:* I could not give him a simple burial, befitting his modest condition.

11.12. *You do not yet know life, how could you know death:* I have already evoked in the Introduction the remarkable comments which this very important statement elicited from Elias Canetti. Here is the entire passage, from Canetti's "Confucius in His Conversations," in *The Conscience of Words* (New York: Seabury, 1979), pages 174–75:

> I know of no sages who took death as seriously as Confucius. He refuses to answer any questions about death. "If one does not yet know life, how should one know death?" No more suitable comment has ever been made on that topic. He knows very well that all such questions refer to a time *after* death. Any answer leaps past death, conjuring away both death and its incomprehensibility. If there is something *afterwards* as there was something *before*, then death loses some of its weight. Confucius refuses to play along with this most unworthy legerdemain. He does not say there is nothing afterwards, he cannot know. But one has the impression that he does not really care about finding out, even if he could. All value is thereby put on life itself; anything of radiance or earnestness that one has taken away from life by putting a good, perhaps the best part of its strength *behind* death is restored to life. Thus, life remains whole, it remains what it is, and even death remains intact, they are not interchangeable, not comparable. They never blend, they are distinct.

11.13. *(The Master said):* these words are not in the original text; most commentators believe that they were accidentally dropped. Some consider that this passage should form an independent section, and not be read as a continuation of 11.13.

A man like Zilu ...: Confucius's statement was prophetic: Zilu died a violent death during the succession struggles in Wei (480 B.C.).

11.14.   *the Long Treasury:* this building had been used as a defensive base by the ruler of Lu, against the ambitious schemings of the Ji Family. Min Ziqian's proposal expressed in an indirect and symbolic way a determination to support faithfully the legitimate authority of the Duke of Lu.

11.15.   *What sort of music is Zilu playing:* literally, "What is Zilu's zithern doing inside my house?" The Master is not objecting to the presence of Zilu's zithern, but to the unsuitable martial tunes which Zilu is playing.

Zilu has ascended to the hall, he has not yet entered the chamber: Zilu is on the right track, but is still far from the goal.

11.18.   *Zigao:* courtesy name of Gao Chai, disciple of Confucius.

extreme: the exact meaning of *bi* is somewhat imprecise: "one-sided," "lacking balance," "prejudiced"?
    Some commentators suggest that this section should be read as a statement made by Confucius, and that the words "The Master said" were accidentally dropped. This hypothesis is consistent with the familiar form of address (personal names) used for all four characters Chai, Shen, Shi and You. (These different forms of address, however, are not reflected in my translation: to avoid confusing readers, every individual is designated throughout under only one name.)

11.19.   *Zigong did not accept his lot ...:* the whole passage is obscure.

11.20. *The-Way-of-the-Good-Man:* seems to refer to a specific doctrine, but we do not know what it was—and the answer of the Master does not clarify the issue.

11.21. *His opinions are sound . . . :* the context of the statement is missing, and we are left with a riddle . . .

11.22. *Zilu asked . . . :* excellent example of the flexible pedagogy of the Master: one should not teach the same thing to different people.

11.23. *The Master was trapped in Kuang:* on this adventure in which Confucius nearly lost his life, see 9.5.

When they were eventually reunited: these words are not in the original text; I have added them for the sake of clarity and logic.

11.25. *You are doing that young man a bad turn:* Confucius felt that this appointment was premature: Zigao should have pursued further studies.

11.26. *Zilu, Zeng Dian, Ran Qiu and Gongxi Chi were sitting with the Master . . . :* the beauty of this long section need not be underlined here—it should be self-evident. Still, it may be useful to add two observations, one on the style, and one on the content of this passage.

Within the *Analects*, the format of this sustained narrative, with dialogues, characters, and subtle psychological hints is quite exceptional; the language itself appears to pertain to a period slightly later than the rest of the book. In the history of Chinese literature, this is the earliest example of what was to become, after many centuries, one of the most exquisite literary *genres*, the short lyrical prose essay.

A superficial acquaintance with the *Analects* has led too many readers to see Confucius as an activist exclusively absorbed by the tasks and responsibilities of public life. We have already had several occasions to challenge such a narrow view, and to point out the strong mystical side which Confucius manifested repeatedly. This aspect of the inner, private Confucius is fully displayed here, in the context of an intimate and informal conversation; in his unexpected support for Zeng Dian's choice, he reveals himself as a man for whom *contemplation* takes precedence over all other values. It is no wonder that, in Song and Ming times, neo-Confucian thinkers under the influence of Chan Buddhism ("Zen")—which they were trying to integrate into Confucianism—attached particular importance to this passage.

Zeng Dian: his courtesy name was Xi; disciple of Confucius, and father of "Master Zeng" (Zeng Shen).

a country not too small: literally, "a country of a thousand chariots" (see note 1.5).

12.1. *restore the rites:* the notion of "rites" or "ritual," which occurs constantly in the *Analects,* is of central importance to Confucian thought. Although for many Western readers it may present a quaint or exotic connotation, it is in fact very much the equivalent of what we simply mean today by "civilization." The concept of civilization is of such universal and permanent relevance, that we hardly realize that the word itself is of fairly recent coinage, and that, at different times, in different cultures, other terms were used in its stead. For instance, as Samuel Johnson was preparing the fourth edition of his great dictionary, he explained to Boswell that "he would not admit *civilization,* but only *civility.*" (Boswell, *Life of Johnson,* entry of March 23, 1772). *Civility,* by the way, could constitute an apt rendition of the Chinese *li,* "rites."

Rites play in civilized society the role that is devolved to *laws* in a social environment where morality has broken down. In this respect, the inflation of legal codification and the multiplication of judicial activity are really a paradoxical measure of the brutalization and moral *lawlessness* of a society. (This paradox seems to have escaped a more activist school of modern Confucianism; the government of Singapore, in its naive but somewhat misguided enthusiasm, recently enacted *laws* to enforce Confucian morality: if they feel neglected by their adult children, parents can now take their unfilial offspring to court!) Hence, the Confucian hostility toward the very concept of law: laws make people cunning, they foster amorality and cynicism, ruthlessness and a perverse spirit of strife and contention.

In this same sense, when Montesquieu observed that "in Europe, most nations are still ruled by social usages *(les mœurs),*" which preserve them from the dangers of anarchy or the brutalities of despotism (*Esprit des lois,* VIII, 8), he was unwittingly expressing a typically Confucian view. Conversely, when a nation needs to be ruled by a plethora of new laws, by a proliferation of minute regulations, amendments, and amendments of amendments, usually it is because it has lost its basic values and is no longer bound by common traditions and civilized conventions. For a society, compulsive lawmaking and constant judicial interventions are a symptom of moral illness.

12.2. *Let no resentment enter public and private affairs:* the phrasing in the original is ambiguous; it can mean either "do not let your own resentments interfere with your management of affairs" or "manage affairs in such a way that you will not create resentment."

12.3. *Sima Niu:* see 12.5.

12.5. *Sima Niu was grieving:* commentators traditionally believed that this Sima Niu was a character of the same name, mentioned in the *Zuo zhuan,* who had several brothers (among whom was the nasty Huan Tui, already encountered in 7.23). If we accept this identification, Sima Niu's complaint could be read as a virtuous way of disclaiming any association with his disreputable brothers, who were guilty of rebellion. Actually there is no evidence to support the theory that Sima Niu of the *Analects* and Sima Niu of the *Zuo zhuan* were the same person. It would be more prudent simply to stick to the terse information provided by Sima Qian's *Shi ji:* "Sima Niu was a disciple of Confucius; his given name was Geng, and courtesy name Ziniu."

This famous passage is at the origin of the common misconception that Confucius said: "All men are brothers." In fact, as the reader can see, the actual statement was slightly different, and it was not made by Confucius himself. (Needless to say, however, this popular notion, even though inaccurate in a narrow sense, did certainly not contradict the spirit of Confucian humanism.)

12.8.   *Ji Zicheng:* an official from Wei country.

Sir, what you have just said is deplorable indeed: this phrase is followed by three words, *jun zi ye,* which I have not translated. Commentators are not sure of what to do with them; three different meanings are conceivable: 1. You speak as a gentleman, but what you just said is deplorable; 2. What you just said regarding the gentleman is deplorable; 3. It is deplorable that you said that, for, when a gentleman has spoken, (even a team of four horses would not be able to retrieve his words). Today, grammarians generally consider that the second reading should be considered the correct one, though the third reading cannot be excluded. They absolutely reject the first reading—which, by the way, was suggested by the great Zhu Xi; of course, Zhu Xi was not a grammarian . . .

without its hair, the skin of a tiger . . . : note that, in Chinese, the word "culture" *(wen)* originally meant "(natural) patterns" such as those formed by hair on the pelt of an animal.

12.10. *Zizhang asked:* the question bears, it seems, on two conventional expressions which Zizhang might have encountered in a text (?). The whole issue is unclear; a similar obscurity is encountered at 12.21.

If not for the sake of wealth . . . : these two verses come from the *Book of Poems* (Poem 188, referring to a woman who suspects that her husband is planning to take a new wife for one of these two reasons). There is no good explanation for the presence of the two verses in this place; they may have been attached to this passage simply through a copying mistake.

12.11. *Let the lord be a lord; the subject a subject; the father a father; the son a son:* this important statement must be interpreted in connection with the precept to "rectify the names" (see note 13.3) which was Confucius's foremost concern.

In the Confucian view, the sociopolitical order rests upon a correct definition of each individual's function, identity, duties, privileges, and responsibilities. It is a teaching that, even today, has lost nothing of its relevance: the moral chaos of our age—with its infantile adults, precociously criminal children, androgynous individuals, homosexual families, despotic leaders, asocial citizens, incestuous fathers, etc.—reflects a collective drift into uncertainty and confusion; obligations attached to specific roles, age differentiations, even sexual identity are no longer perceived clearly. Before this alarming situation, anthropologists, sociologists, and psychologists are now rediscovering the *need for rituals* and the importance of role definitions, to ensure the harmonious integration of the individual into society. See, for instance, the writings of Claude Lévi-Strauss or, more recently, of Boris Cyrulnik. At times, their views sound like a downright echo of the *Analects.* Here is Boris Cyrulnik, in an interview published in *Le Nouvel Observateur* (no 1517, December 2 and 9, 1993; my translation):

When families are no longer able to generate rites that can interpret the surrounding world and transmit the parental culture, children find themselves cut off from reality, and they have to create their own culture—a culture of archaic violence which they themselves cannot manage...

Incidences of incest are increasing because too many men no longer feel that they are fathers. As family relationships have weakened and roles have changed, individuals do not see clearly what their proper place is. This is the symptom of a cultural breakdown.

12.12. *Zilu never slept over a promise:* he never postponed its execution till the next day.

12.13. *I would prefer to make lawsuits unnecessary:* on the repugnance for judicial interventionism, see note 12.1. Later on, this attitude continued to inform Confucian practice under the Empire. For instance, a prefect who had adjudicated a great many lawsuits during the time of his posting could not expect to be commended for his zeal; the likelihood was that he would be badly noted by his superiors: so much contentiousness among the people under his authority, reflected poorly on the quality of his administration. (Actually, in this respect, he might have better employed his time simply writing poetry or playing the zither in the moonlight.)

12.15. *A gentleman enlarges his learning...:* repeats 6.27 with a slight variation.

12.17. *To govern is to be straight:* one could also translate: "politics is rectitude." The two words are homophonous *(zheng).* As we have already seen, puns play an important role in ancient Chinese thought.

12.19. *The moral power of the gentleman is wind, the moral power of the common man is grass. Under the wind the grass must* *bend:* this statement was to have huge historical implications, as it was invoked through the ages to justify the authority of the ruling classes. It contributed powerfully to make Confucianism unpopular with all modern democrats.

12.20. *cut from straight timber:* literally, "made from straight stuff." (I could not resist borrowing Kant's vivid image: "Out of timber so crooked as that from which man is made, nothing entirely straight can be built.")

examine men's words . . . the necessity of deferring to others: this is Waley's rendition; its elegance and precision cannot be improved upon.

12.22. *Raise the straight:* repeats 2.19.

13.3. *to rectify the names:* this concern pervades all the *Analects:* it sums up the whole Confucian enterprise. The correct use of language is the basis on which the sociopolitical order is built. Note that, here, my translation is literal, whereas in the Introduction I referred to this same passage in the form of a free paraphrase.

13.4. *Fan Chi asked Confucius to teach him agronomy:* instead of seeking from Confucius the humanistic *education* which only the Master could impart, Fan Chi asks him to waste his time providing a technological *training* which could easily, and more appropriately, be obtained elsewhere. As common sense clearly indicates, this passage merely underlines Fan Chi's fatuousness, but modern critics have found in it damning evidence that Confucianism stifled the development of science and technology in China.

An examination of the cultural factors that may have inhibited scientific inquiry in China is obviously beyond the scope of this note. Let us merely point out here that the fashionable anti-Confucian prejudice evoked above is predicated upon what could be called "the Snow Fallacy"—i.e., a belief in the existence of "Two Cultures" which, competing for our minds and attention, are being separated by a widening gap across which bridges ought urgently to be built. C. P. Snow (whose mind was no less vulgar than Fan Chi's) assumed, in his notorious Rede Lecture of 1961, an equivalence between cultural experience and scientific information—as if any meaningful equation could be drawn between, on the one hand, the understanding of Shakespeare, and, on the other, the awareness of the second law of thermodynamics. To advocate linking the development of human consciousness to the storage of technical knowledge seems as pertinent as to prescribe hearing aids for the soul, or reading glasses for the mind. (Snow's original lecture, *The Two Cultures*, was reissued by Cambridge University Press, 1994; for an eloquent refutation of Snow's thesis, see F. R. Leavis: *Two Cultures? The Significance of C. P. Snow* [London: Chatto and Windus, 1962].)

People would flock from everywhere with their babies strapped to their backs: in Confucius's time, the power and the prosperity of a state were directly dependent upon the size of its mostly peasant population. The peasants formed a mass of taxpayers and of potential soldiers. But, as they were not in bondage to the land, when they were dissatisfied with their government, they still had the recourse of "voting with their feet": mass migration was the ultimate sanction of political life—the virtue and political wisdom of a prince could be measured by the number of subjects he managed to attract and retain on his lands. (See also 13.9 and 13.16.)

13.5. *repartee:* as I have already indicated (see note 2.2), all diplomatic exchanges were conducted through a formal *découpage* of quotations borrowed from the *Poems*.

13.7. *Lu and Wei are brothers:* commentators have developed various interpretations of this statement. Confucius was perhaps comparing the decadence and disorder which were affecting both countries at the time.

13.8. *Prince Jing of Wei:* he had a reputation for virtue. It seems that Confucius praised him here for his moderation: at each stage, he expressed greater satisfaction than his actual situation warranted.

13.9. *So many people:* see note 13.4. An important statement: if culture is the crowning achievement of a good government it can only intervene after material prosperity has been secured.

13.13. *steer straight . . . the tasks of government:* once more, this statement is based on a pun: "steer straight" and "government" are homophonous *(zheng).*

13.14. *Ran Qiu was returning from court:* Ran Qiu was employed by the Ji family, which had actually usurped political power. For Confucius, the authority of the Ji was illegitimate, and therefore Ran Qiu's activity could not truly constitute a governmental responsibility.

13.16. *Make the local people happy . . . :* see note 13.4.

13.17. *Jufu:* a town in Lu.

13.18. *Men of integrity do things differently:* this is a fundamental statement of Confucian humanism. Its importance did not escape the early enemies of Confucianism. The Legalist philosophers (especially Han Feizi, in the third century B.C.) who developed the theory of the totalitarian state with a ruthless logic and an intellectual brilliance never equaled since (not even by the ideologies of the twentieth century), focused on this passage, pointing out that humanism was a form of corruption that threatened the integrity of the state.

On the conflict between private and public loyalties, the Confucian position is vulnerable to the attacks of unfair critics; yet, to the unprejudiced mind, it presents a complex subtlety

("There is integrity in what they do") that should resist polemical distortion. One is reminded of E. M. Forster's provocative affirmation of the primacy of personal relations, which was also to become eventually an object of derision in the light of later political scandals—though it remains worth pondering in its full context:

> I do not believe in Belief . . . I have, however, to live in an Age of Faith . . . It is extremely unpleasant really. It is bloody in every sense of the word. And I have to keep my end up in it. Where do I start? With personal relationships. Here is something comparatively solid in a world full of violence and cruelty . . . Starting from [personal relationships], I get a little order into the contemporary chaos. One must be fond of people and trust them if one is not to make a mess of life . . . Personal relations are despised today. They are regarded as bourgeois luxuries, as products of a time of fair weather which is now past, and we are urged to get rid of them, and to dedicate ourselves to some movement or cause instead. I hate the idea of causes, and if I had to choose between betraying my country and betraying my friend, I hope I should have the guts to betray my country. Such a choice may scandalize the modern reader, and he may stretch his patriotic hand to the telephone at once and ring up the police. It would not have shocked Dante, though. Dante places Brutus and Cassius in the lowest circle of Hell because they had chosen to betray their friend Julius Caesar rather than their country Rome . . . Love and loyalty to an individual can run counter to the claims of the State. When they do—down with the State, say I, which means that the State would down me. (E. M. Forster, "What I Believe," in *Two Cheers for Democracy* [Harmondsworth: Penguin, 1972] 75–77).

13.21.   *If I cannot find people who steer a middle course to associate with:* this is Waley's rendition; I part from his interpretation, however, in the remainder of the passage.

the crazy and the pure: the two words *kuang juan* have raised many questions. Either they mean one and the same type of person, "crazy-impetuous" (Waley's interpretation), or they mean two extreme opposites; this reading (which I have adopted here) finds its main justification in Mencius, and is followed by most Chinese commentators.

13.22. *a shaman:* although the gist of the passage is clear (the importance of steadfastness), its actual formulation has given rise to different interpretations: it all depends on the exact meaning of *wu yi:* "diviners and doctors," "shaman"—or "quack." Either, 'steadfastness is such an important virtue, that Southerners insist on it as a prerequisite for their holy leaders.' Or, 'steadfastness is such an important virtue, that even Southern Barbarians demand it—even from their quacks.'

On the statement in The Changes: I have supplied these words to make explicit the meaning of the passage. Confucius is commenting here on the text pertaining to the third line of the 32nd hexagram in the *Book of Changes.*

13.27. *silence:* see 12.3: "He who practices humanity is reluctant to speak."

14.1. *When the Way prevails in the state, serve it . . . :* what is translated here by "serve" *(gu),* means more literally: "to accept rewards, to draw an official salary. Compare this passage with 8.13.

14.5. *Yi* and *Ao:* mythical heroes. Regarding Ao, this passage alludes to some nautical feat *(dang zhou),* the actual meaning of which is not clear. "Good sailor" is a free adaptation.

Yu and *Ji:* legendary characters from the third millennium B.C. Yu (see 8.18) saved the world from the deluge, and Ji invented agriculture. The achievements of Yu and Ji established the first foundations of civilization, and are being contrasted here with the violent and purely physical feats of Yi and Ao.

14.6. *Gentlemen:* as it has been repeatedly underlined previously, one of Confucius's most revolutionary innovations was to replace the notion of *social* aristocracy with that of *moral* aristocracy. In a few occurrences, however, such as this passage, the word "gentleman" is still used in its original acceptation of "member of the nobility," "aristocrat".

14.8. *Pi Chen, Shi Shu, Ziyu:* high officials in the country of Zheng; they were assistants of the prime minister, Zichan—a statesman whom Confucius admired.

14.9. *Zichan was a generous man:* Confucius brings here a corrective to the traditional image of Zichan as a man of great severity.

Zixi: there were three different characters with this name; one of them was a cousin of Zichan, the other two were aristocrats from Chu country. It is difficult to determine which one is being referred to in this passage.

Guan Zhong: see note 3.22.

14.11. *Meng Gongchuo:* grand officer in Lu country.

great family: literally, "Zhao or Wei."

small state: literally, "Teng or Xue."

14.12. *Zang Wuzhong:* grand officer in Lu country, famous for his sagacity (one example of which can be found in *Zuo zhuan*).

Zhuangzi: from Lu country, famous for his valor.

14.13. *Gongshu Wenzi:* grand officer from Wei.

Was that so? Could that really have been so?: it is generally understood that the first question expresses admiration, and the second one, doubt—"All this is admirable—if it is true."

14.14. *Zang Wuzhong occupied Fang:* this episode is reported in *Zuo zhuan* (23d year of Duke Xiang).

14.16. *When Duke Huan killed Prince Jiu:* this episode is reported in *Zuo zhuan* (8th and 9th year of Duke Zhuang). Shao Hu and Guan Zhong were both serving Jiu. When his brother Huan killed him in order to take the throne, Shao Hu committed suicide out of loyalty to Jiu, whereas Guan Zhong offered his services to the usurper.

One of the prince's tutors ... but the other: these words are not in the original; I have supplied them to make the meaning explicit.

14.18. *thanks to his master:* these words are not in the original. I have supplied them to explain the point.

14.19. *Kong Yu:* see note 5.15.

Tuo: see note 6.16.

Wangsun Jia: see note 3.13.

14.20. *A promise easily made:* this saying might also refer to imprudent claims or boasts that one cannot easily live up to.

14.21. *Confucius made a ritual ablution and went to court:* Confucius was no longer in office, but he still enjoyed a formal rank—hence he felt morally obliged to make a statement in this distressing affair (which is reported in *Zuo zhuan,* 14th year of Duke Ai). The Three Lords were the heads of the great families who had virtually usurped the political authority of the Duke. Confucius feared that they might eventually do to the Duke of Lu what Chen Heng had just done to the Duke of Qi—hence his sense of frustration and despair when the Duke of Lu simply tells him to refer the matter to the Three Lords. It is only out of principle that Confucius goes through these various steps: he can entertain no illusions regarding the actual use of this initiative: he truly is "the one who keeps pursuing what he knows to be impossible" (14.38).

14.22. *Tell him the truth, even if it offends him:* another interpretation is also possible: "If you oppose him, do it loyally."

14.25. *Qu Boyu:* grand officer in Wei. Confucius was once his guest.

What a messenger: some traditional commentators believe that Confucius is favorably impressed by the modesty and moral subtlety of the messenger (who does not speak of "not making mistakes", but of "making fewer mistakes"). Waley, on the contrary, has wondered if Confucius was not being ironic.

14.26. *He who holds no official position discusses no official policies:* repeats 8.14, but here I have used a slightly different phrasing in English. (Actually, I felt strongly tempted to translate: "He who is not in the driver's seat should not discuss the driving." But I was afraid that the modern tone of this rendition might sound a jarring note—which is a pity, considering that it is remarkably close to the actual wording of the original.)

14.30. *It is not your obscurity that should distress you:* repeats the first part of 1.16. The second part of the passage is different.

14.32. *Hey, you!:* this is a free transposition, in an attempt to convey the utter rudeness of Weisheng Mu: in the original, he addresses Confucius by calling him *Qiu* (his personal name, which could only be used by his parents and elders, and was taboo for anyone else). Weisheng Mu must be a hermit who rejected society and all its conventions; in his eyes, Confucius's wanderings from court to court are motivated by a frivolous desire to display his political eloquence. Confucius explains that these successive moves are forced upon him by the deafness of his listeners; he has to continue his search for a responsive audience.

14.33. *Ji:* legendary horse, which could run a thousand miles in one day.

14.36. *Gongbo Liao:* from Lu country; according to a tradition, he may have been a disciple of Confucius.

Ji Sun: member of the powerful Ji family.

Zifu Jingbo: grand officer in Lu.

14.37. *The highest wisdom . . . :* it seems that this passage deals with the various strategies which a sage should adopt when facing the hostility of a ruler; the main thing is not to expose oneself to an explicit condemnation ("certain words")—which should already be displayed in "certain attitudes."

Seven men did this: this phrase is puzzling; it seems to have been accidentally interrupted. It may not even pertain to the preceding passage, and its presence here appears quite arbitrary.

14.39. *A man carrying a basket:* probably another hermit, as his bold and unconventional comments would suggest. Some bits of Daoist propaganda, directed against Confucianism, paradoxically found their way into the *Analects* (we shall find a few more of these later on). They usually follow the same pattern: Confucius finds himself confronted with some disconcerting and formidable eccentric, who outwits him and whose wisdom leaves him speechless.

If the water of the ford is deep . . . : these two verses are from the *Book of Poems* (Poem 34). Instead of "Wade through it with your clothes on," one may also encounter the interpretation "use the stepping stones." It all depends upon the meaning of the character *li*, on which there is no general agreement. (The reader who feels perplexed by this sort of discussion might find some solace in reading again Borges's comments. See note 1.13).

14.40. *King Gaozong:* reigned at the end of the fourteenth and beginning of the thirteenth century B.C. (Shang dynasty). During the mourning period, the new king did not appoint new officials and all affairs were conducted by the old administration of the dead king.

14.43. *Yuan Rang:* traditionally identified as an old friend of Confucius; he must have been a rather eccentric character. According to the *Book of Rites,* when Yuan Rang's mother died, Confucius, who had arrived to help with the funeral, found him singing merrily by the side of the coffin.

In fact, this passage and the following one deal with the incorrect behavior of young people in front of their elders.

15.1. *military tactics:* military matters were beneath the attention of a Confucian gentleman. This attitude passed into the popular mentality—witness the familiar proverb: "One does not turn good iron into nails, one does not turn good men into soldiers."

15.3. *I have one single thread:* see 4.15.

15.5. *to govern by inactivity:* one could also translate "by non-interference". This ancient political ideal was to be more systematically developed by the Daoist philosophers.

"Inactivity" should not be taken as a form of apathy—on the contrary, it represents a superior type of activity: the most efficient action is the one that uses the least energy, and when *no* energy is being spent at all, efficiency is supreme.

In Confucian politics, however, the dynamics of "inactivity" pertain to ethics: the ruler governs purely by setting a moral example, and his virtue radiates down to the people.

facing south: position of the sovereign. Imperial palaces of later periods strictly followed this tradition and were always built on a north-south axis. (The Forbidden City in Peking remains today a superb example of this cosmic conception: the imperial throne is the hub of the universe.)

15.7.   *Shi Yu:* a grand officer from Wei.

Qu Boyu: see note 14.25. The Chinese language has no tenses: it is uncertain whether Confucius's comment should be expressed in the present or in the past—both men lived in the same period.

15.9.   *there are instances where he will give his life in order to fulfill his humanity:* this very important statement was often invoked through the ages, mostly in connection with the moral obligation of political dissent. For a Confucian gentleman, the duty of obedience to the prince was relative, whereas the obligation of fidelity to his own humanity was absolute. Xun Zi (c. 298–235 B.C.)—he was the third great Confucian thinker after Confucius and Mencius, and the last master of the Confucian school in the pre-imperial period—would eventually sum it up with terse eloquence: "A minister follows the Way, he does not follow the ruler."

15.11.   *the calendar of Xia:* according to traditional commentators, this most ancient calendar followed more closely the seasons, and therefore was of greater use for the peasants than the more artificial calendars of subsequent dynasties.

the chariot of Yin: it was made of wood; Confucius allegedly praised the austere simplicity of its making, in contrast with the more precious and elaborate materials that were used later on.

the cap of Zhou: it was much more elaborate than the one used under the earlier dynasties. When it came to ritual and culture, Confucius was not averse to pomp and splendor.

the Coronation Hymn of Shun and the Victory Hymn of Wu: see 3.25 and 7.14, as well as the note for 3.25.

Proscribe the music of Zheng: Tolstoy, who read the *Analects* many times over the years, repeatedly expressed in his diaries his admiration for Confucius who, in his wisdom, saw the need to keep the awesome power of music under strict state control. (I am not sure, however, if the Kreutzer Sonata was really a latter-day manifestation of the music of Zheng!)

15.13. *I have never seen a man who loved virtue as much as sex:* repeats 9.18.

15.14. *Zang Sunchen:* see note 5.18.

Liuxia Hui: talented and virtuous man from Lu; actually, his real name was Zhan Huo, or Zhan Ji.

15.19. *A gentleman resents his incompetence; he does not resent his obscurity:* on the same topic—far away across time and space—La Bruyère was to make a similar observation: "Nous devons travailler à nous rendre très dignes de quelque emploi: le reste ne nous regarde point, c'est l'affaire des autres." (*Les Caractères,* "Du mérite personnel.") (We must endeavor to become fully worthy of an official position; the rest does not concern us, it is other people's business.)

15.20. *A gentleman worries lest he might disappear from this world without having made a name for himself:* in ancient and classical China, to achieve fame was a moral imperative (an equivalent of this mentality can be found in the culture of the Italian Renaissance). The only form of life after death was to survive in the minds of posterity; the only form of immortality was the one granted by historical memory. (I have touched upon these notions in an essay "The Chinese Attitude Towards the Past" in *Papers on Far Eastern History,* 39, March 1989, to be reissued in my forthcoming collection, *Detours*).

It might appear at first as if, in this statement, Confucius was contradicting 15.19, "A gentleman resents his incompetence, *he does not resent his obscurity*". In fact, there is no contradiction: according to the fearsome Confucian optimism, if a gentleman remains unknown, it can only be *because* he is incompetent: genuine merit is bound to be recognized sooner or later. If he eventually disappears without having achieved fame, the fault must be entirely his—his failure must merely sanction his lack of talent.

Throughout most of his career, and in spite of all rebuffs and tribulations, Confucius retained an unshakable faith in his political destiny. It was only at the end of his life, when he realized that his time was nearly over and that he would not be afforded a chance to fulfill his Heavenly mission, that he began to contemplate the mystery of failure and the possibility—as it must have then appeared to him—that virtue may ultimately meet with the absurd scandal of its own defeat.

15.24. *Reciprocity:* see also 6.30 and 4.15.

15.25. *The people of today . . . :* for this last sentence, there are various interpretations, but none is fully convincing. The *Three Dynasties* are Xia, Shang, and Zhou, the earliest dynasties of China.

15.26. *Scribes encountering a doubtful word would leave a blank space:* the word "doubtful" is not in the original text, but it is generally supplied by commentators and translators in order to make the meaning explicit. D. C. Lau (following a suggestion of Chow Tse-tsung) adopted a completely different interpretation (which is legitimate philologically): "Scribes lacked refinement." The next sentence is then supposed to illustrate this "lack of refinement": "Owners of horses would permit others to drive them." But it is difficult to see how the sharing of horses would betray a lack of refinement. Furthermore, the

Lau-Chow reading would imply that *modern* usages are better than *ancient* ones: such a view is hardly conceivable in a Confucian perspective, and has no equivalent in the entire *Analects*.

This statement seems in fact to be simply in praise of prudence: on matters that are doubtful, one should reserve judgment. (See, for instance, 2.18).

15.28.   *When everyone dislikes a man . . . :* I am simply reproducing Waley's rendition: its concision and accuracy cannot be improved upon.

15.33.   *The power:* the original text merely says "it," but the context makes it fairly clear that "power," or "political authority," is the subject of this statement.

15.39.   *My teaching is addressed to all indifferently:* one could also translate: *Education obliterates all distinctions.* This famous and extremely important statement summed up for millions of readers through the centuries one of the most progressive and revolutionary aspects of Confucius's thought: education should be open to all, without any distinction of birth, rank, or social or economic status. Actually, Confucius's disciples came from the most diverse backgrounds and presented remarkably dissimilar and uneven aptitudes: the only requirement they had to meet at the start was to demonstrate a genuine passion for learning.

Although other passages in the *Analects* (see for instance 7.7) and the historical practice of the Confucian school all confirm the impressive reality of this commitment to universal education, the statement which we are considering here may well have originally had a quite different meaning, which some modern Western translators have preferred to the traditional Chinese interpretation. This modern foreign reading ("among people, there are differences in education, but none in kind") can find some grammatical support; nevertheless, it remains devoid of *historical* weight, since it was not in that sense that it left its imprint and exerted its influence upon the Chinese mind during the last two thousand years.

15.41.   *Words are merely for communication:* Emerson said, "All language is vehicular and transitive, and is good, as ferries and horses are, for conveyance, and not as farms and houses are, for homestead." But then, he was familiar with the *Analects*, which he first read in an early English translation by Joshua Marshman (printed by the missionary press of Serampore, 1809), and again in David Collie's translation of the *Four Books* (Malacca, 1828). He communicated his interest in Confucian thought to Thoreau, who, in *Walden*, quoted repeatedly from Confucius and Mencius. (On Emerson's Confucian readings, see R. D. Richardson, *Emerson: The Mind on Fire* [Berkeley: University of California, 1995], 219, 349, 392.)

15.42.   *The blind music master:* I have supplied the word blind, which is not in the original, to enable the reader to grasp the situation evoked in this passage. Traditionally, music masters were blind.

16.1. *Our ancient kings established Zhuanyu as an autonomous domain:* literally, "our ancient kings granted Zhuanyu the right to offer sacrifices to Mount Dongmeng."

Zhou Ren: an ancient sage, of uncertain identification.

Zhuanyu . . . is close to our master's castle: literally, "Zhuanyu is close to Bi." (Bi was the stronghold of the Ji Family.)

not poverty but inequality . . . : in this whole passage, I have not followed the exact word order of the original, which seems to have been jumbled.

16.3. *The Ducal House of Lu has lost its authority:* it has lost the *lu*, i.e., the power, either of appointing officials or of drawing income from state levies. (The former meaning seems the most likely.)

16.8. *great men:* who have either high authority or high morality.

16.11. *I have heard this saying and I have seen it practiced:* I have restored the logical order between these two phrases, which seems to have been accidentally reversed in the original text.

16.12. *Boyi and Shuqi starved in the wilderness:* literally, they starved "at the foot of Mount Shouyang." For Boyi and Shuqi, see note 5.23.

Is this not an illustration of what was just said: the passage is corrupt; some commentators believe that this phrase refers to 16.11. It seems more likely that 16.12 lost its beginning.

16.13. *Chen Ziqin:* in this passage, he is designated under his original name, Chen Gang; see note 1.10.

Confucius's son: Kong Li. In the original text, Chen Ziqin calls him by his courtesy name, Boyu.

I was discreetly crossing the courtyard: literally, "I was crossing the courtyard with quickened steps"—as a conventional mark of respect.

16.14. *Various titles are used: ... :* this passage probably belonged to some handbook of ceremonial, and must have been inserted here by accident.

17.1. *Yang Huo:* steward of the Ji Family. In the first stage of decline from the feudal order, ducal authority had been usurped by the heads of the great families, and then it fell in turn into the hands of their stewards. We have just learned (16.2) what were Confucius's views on this alarming development, and therefore it is easy to understand why he was unwilling to see Yang Huo. The latter attempted to force a meeting by offering him a present: every gift created a ritual obligation for the beneficiary to acknowledge it with a visit.

At the end of the passage, Confucius's agreement remains ambiguous.

17.4. *Wucheng, where Ziyou was governor:* the words "where Ziyou was governor" are not in the original; educated Chinese readers were naturally aware of this information.

the sound of stringed instruments and hymns: indicating a ritual ceremony that was performed with a solemnity completely out of proportion with these humble surroundings. At first, Confucius is amused by Ziyou's excessive zeal, but eventually he sees his disciple's point—which was also Chesterton's: "All the exaggerations are right if they exaggerate the right thing" ("On Gargoyles," in *Alarms and Discursions* [London, 1910]).

17.5.   *Gongshan Furao:* steward of the Ji Family, of which Bi was the stronghold. His rebellion was directed against Lord Ji; Confucius could therefore believe that it might provide him with an opportunity to restore the legitimate authority of the Duke of Lu.

establish a new Zhou dynasty in the East: Zhou had originally developed in Western China; the country of Lu (in today's Shandong Province), where Confucius lived, was in Eastern China. Confucius is making here a very clear statement on what he believes to be his lofty historical mission.

17.7.   *Bi Xi:* governor of Zhongmou, and steward of a great family in the state of Jin.

17.8.   *The love of humanity without the love of learning degenerates into silliness:* whoever doubts the permanent relevance of this observation should take a look today at the antics of all varieties of well-meaning but ignorant activism currently in fashion! Uninformed kindness can cause more havoc than deliberate mischievousness; but, by a strange logic, it is too often assumed that kindness should by itself carry a sort of automatic dispensation from intelligence—whereas these two qualities are in fact organically related. "Natural kindness is rare, *only intelligence can produce kindness,*" Jules Renard wrote (*Journal,* entry of 5 April 1903); the same idea was repeatedly developed by Proust. And Unamuno castigated Cervantes for having written that Sancho "was a good man, but had no brains"—as if kindness and stupidity were compatible: "One cannot be foolish, yet good." (Miguel de Unamuno: *Vida de Don Quijote y Sancho,* I, 7).

17.10.   *his son:* literally, Boyu.

the first and the second part of the Poems: literally, *Zhou nan* and *Shao nan.*

17.11.   *as if ritual merely meant . . . :* see 3.3.

17.17.   *Clever talk . . . :* repeats 1.3.

17.18.   *purple:* an intermediary color, whereas vermilion is a primary color. The whole passage seems to refer to the complexity that perverts simplicity.

popular music: literally, "the music of Zheng," already condemned above, 15.11.

17.19.   *I wish to speak no more:* for further comments on this splendid passage, see the introduction, "The Silences of Confucius."

The concept of teaching without words was more commonly cultivated within the Daoist tradition (see for instance Lao Zi: "He who speaks does not know, he who knows does not speak.") It was further developed by the Chan (Zen) school of Buddhism. Chan was brought to China in 520 A.D. by the Indian missionary Bodhidharma, who, according to a later Scripture, belonged to a tradition that went back to Buddha's disciple Kasyapa: one day, instead of preaching, Buddha silently plucked a flower and smiled. Only Kasyapa understood this wordless communication, and in turn, using a similar method, passed it on to his own disciples—thus establishing the transmission of the Chan teaching.

Nietzsche would have appreciated this statement of Confucius—since he wrote (in *La Gaya Scienza*, IV, 340) that he "admired the courage and wisdom of Socrates in all he did, said, *and did not say,*" but also that he "would have admired Socrates even more, *had he remained silent in the last moments of his life.*"

17.20.   *Ru Bei:* a character from the country of Lu, on whom next to nothing is known.

Confucius declines the invitation on the unimpeachable grounds of illness; but simultaneously makes it perfectly clear that he is *not* ill. Polite insult may be more prudent, but it is also the supreme form of insult; it appears here that Confucius was also a great master of this subtle art.

17.21.   *Zai Yu:* he had some talent, but in the very area which Confucius distrusted—eloquence (see 11.3). To Confucius, Zai Yu's general performance was usually distasteful (see for instance 3.21 and 5.10)—suggesting a type of mind that has become all too common in our modern culture, the "specialized brute."

Three years mourning for one's parents: normally the person who was in mourning suspended all his usual activities, and even abandoned his residence and moved to a hut erected for this purpose, next to the parent's grave. The obligation to observe a long retreat at the death of a parent remained in force for the ruling elite during the entire imperial history of China. Incidentally, this custom had a beneficial effect upon Chinese culture: members of the scholarly class, thus suddenly freed in mid-career from the busy concerns of government and politics, often used these enforced "sabbatical leaves" to cultivate at leisure, and with much fruit, philosophical, literary, and artistic pursuits.

a new lighter: another variety of wood was ritually used to light the new fire at the beginning of each season.

after only one year: these four words are not in the original text.

17.22.   *play chess:* in Chinese, *bo yi,* which means either "to play chess" or "the game of *bo* and the game of *yi*" (the former being a game of dice, the actual rules of which are not known any more.) The chess to which Confucius refers here *(yi)* is of course not the Persian game which has spread all over the world (a variant of which was introduced later on in China, and is called *xiang qi* in modern Chinese). *Yi* (modern Chinese: *wei qi*) is pronounced *go* in Japanese, and under the latter name it has recently begun to enjoy some popularity in the West.

17.23. *a vulgar man who is brave but not just may become a bandit:* Thomas More expressed a similar idea: "Theft comes easier to a man of spirit." (*Utopia*, Book 1).

17.25. *Women and underlings:* literally "women and vulgar men." Contrary to what is often mistakenly assumed, Confucius was not making here a universal statement that would lump all women in the same category as "vulgar men." Actually, the very wording of the original text (*yang*, here translated as "to handle," means literally "to educate," "to feed," "to keep," "to raise," "to nourish") indicates that Confucius's observation merely addressed the narrow and specific context of *the household*. For the head of a large family clan gathered in the same compound, relations with the female members of the household and the domestic staff do pose delicate problems of management and authority.

Now, what was Confucius's attitude toward women? No conclusion can be drawn from this passage, which is not directed at the issue of women in general—and there are no other clues to be found on this question in the *Analects*. Although it would be unfair to accuse Confucius of prejudice on the basis of this single statement (which, within its particular context, presents an observation that is sensible and psychologically shrewd), it would also be silly to expect that, in his view of women, Confucius might have departed significantly from the mentality of his time. The great classical scholar Paul Veyne, in a recent summing up of his experiences as an historian of Ancient Rome, forcefully reminded us that the fundamental beliefs of each age—those which usually remain unsaid—are never challenged at the time, for they are self-evident, and no one perceives that they are mere assumptions; thus, for instance, the institution of slavery was not questioned in antiquity, not even by the Stoics or by the early Christians: "No man can think no matter what no matter when." (Paul Veyne, *Le Quotidien et l'intéressant* [Paris: Les Belles Lettres, 1995], 205: "L'homme ne peut penser n'importe quoi n'importe quand.")

18.1.   *the tyrant:* this word is not in the original text, which merely says "him." The character in question is Zhouxin, last king of the Shang (or Yin) Dynasty, who was notorious for his depravity and his ferocity. The Lord of Wei was his stepbrother; the Lord of Ji and Bi Gan were his uncles.

18.2.   *Liuxia Hui:* see 15.14, text and note.

18.4.   *Lord Ji Huan:* the father of Ji Kang.

18.5.   *Jieyu, the Madman of Chu:* Jieyu, as well as the various hermits whom we shall meet below (18.6 and 18.7) are the rather subversive products of the Daoist imagination, who have infiltrated the *Analects,* where they play the role of an anti-Confucian "fifth column."

18.6.   *Confucius sighed:* the eremitic ideal is certainly attractive; Marcus Aurelius (whose thoughts are sometimes reminiscent of Confucian wisdom—no wonder modern Chinese scholars read the *Meditations* with attention and sympathy) faced the same temptation: "Men seek for seclusion in the wilderness, by the seashore, or in the mountains—a dream you have cherished only too fondly yourself. But such fancies are wholly unworthy of a philosopher" (*Meditations,* IV, 3).

18.8.   *Boyi and Shuqi:* see 5.23, 7.15, and 16.12.

Yuzhong, Yiyi, Zhuzhang, and Shaolian: these characters cannot be identified with any certainty.

they gave up speech: another interpretation is possible, conveying the opposite meaning: "they became carefree in their speech."

18.9.   *Zhi, the grand music master . . . :* these court musicians have not been identified, and we do not know what sort of political upheaval caused their exile. In its enigmatic terseness, the whole passage suggests the cultural desolation which followed the fall of a dynasty.

19.2. *should we really say that . . . :* my translation of this last sentence is rather free, but I see no other way to make sense of it.

19.3. *If I have vast wisdom, whom should I not tolerate?:* it is a mark of mediocrity to find other people mediocre. Pascal noted it: "The more intelligent one is, the more men of originality one finds. Ordinary people find no difference between men." (*Pensées,* Kaplan ed., 1444; Lafuma ed., 510.)

19.4. *minor disciplines:* literally "small ways"—i.e., specialized competences, which, for the Confucian humanist, constitute byways that risk diverting him from the universal Way. On this point, see 2.12, text and note.

19.8. *A vulgar man always tries to cover up his mistakes:* other interpretations are possible—see Waley's, for instance: "When the small man goes wrong, *it is always on the side of over-elaboration.*"

19.13. *leisure:* note that more traditional translations usually prefer to put "left-over energy"; yet "leisure" has both philological and philosophical support. This notion *(you)* is very similar to what the ancient Greeks called *scholê* (σχολη) to describe the state of a person who belongs to himself, who has free disposition of himself. (The Greek word *scholê* means not only rest or leisure, but also the way in which leisure is used: study, learning; by extension, it designates as well the place where study and learning are conducted: study-room or school. The English "school" derives, through Old French and Latin, from *scholê*.)

From this passage, we see that, in the Confucian perspective, both politics and culture are the offspring of leisure; therefore, they are the province of the gentleman, who alone possesses free time. The same view was developed in Classical Greece. In one of Plato's dialogues, Socrates asks: "Are we slaves, or do we have leisure?" Bernard Knox has commented: "Leisure was regarded as the indispensable condition of the good life and the characteristic condition of free men. 'Slaves,' so ran a Greek proverb, 'have no leisure'—it was a definition". From Greece, the notion passed to Rome: the very concept of "liberal arts" *(artes liberales)* embodies the association between cultural pursuits and the condition of the free man *(liber)*—as opposed to the slave (whose skills pertain to the lower sphere of practical activity, *technê* ($\tau\epsilon\chi\nu\eta$). (See Bernard Knox, *The Oldest Dead White European Males and Other Reflections on the Classics* [New York: Norton, 1993], 79, 104.)

These views were maintained in European culture. Samuel Johnson was merely stating the evidence of common sense when he observed that "All intellectual improvement arises from leisure." (Boswell, *Life of Johnson*, entry of April 13, 1773). But one century later, Nietzsche was to note the erosion of civilized leisure under what he considered to be a deleterious American influence:

> There is something barbarous, characteristic of "Redskin" blood, in the American thirst for gold. Their restless urge for work—which is the typical vice of the New World—is now barbarizing old Europe by contamination, and is fostering here a

sterility of the mind that is most extraordinary. Already, we
are ashamed of leisure; lengthy meditation becomes practically
a cause for remorse ... "Do anything rather than do nothing":
this principle is the rope with which all superior forms of culture
and taste are going to be strangled ... It may come to a point
where no one will yield to an inclination for *vita contemplativa*
without having an uneasy conscience and feeling full of self-
contempt. And yet, in the past, the opposite was true: a man of
noble origin, when necessity compelled him to work, would hide
this shameful fact, and the slave worked with the feeling that his
activity was essentially despicable. (*La Gaya Scienza*, IV, 329)

Now, the great paradox of our age, of course, is that,
whereas the wretched *lumpenproletariat* is cursed with the
enforced leisure of large-scale, permanent unemployment,
members of the educated elite, whose liberal professions have
been turned into senseless money-making machines, are con-
demning themselves to the slavery of endless working hours,
day and night, without respite—till they collapse like over-
loaded beasts of burden.

19.18. *Lord Meng Zhuang:* son of Lord Meng Xian, grand
officer of Lu country.

19.20. *Zhouxin:* see note 18.1.

public opinion: these two words are not in the original; I have
supplied them to clarify the meaning of the passage.

19.23. *Shusun Wushu:* grand officer of Lu country.

the hundred apartments: "the hundred *guan*." The original meaning of *guan* is "apartment"; the derived meaning is "official"
(or "ministrant," "civil servant"). Both meanings are encountered in the *Analects*, but most commentators believe that it is
the former that should be adopted here.

19.25. *Chen Ziqin:* see 1.10 and 16.13.

20.1. *Yao said . . . :* for the most part, section 20.1 is a patch-work of ill-connected archaic fragments, which are somewhat related in their language and contents to the *Book of Documents* (a compilation of edicts and admonitions from the early rulers and their wise ministers). These texts were used as teaching materials in the Confucian school, which may explain how they found their way into the *Analects*. (This hypothesis was advanced by D. C. Lau).

From *Set standards for weights and measures* on, it seems that we are back to the original *Analects*.

20.2. *What are the Four Evils . . . :* for the description of the Four Evils, what I am offering here is more a free adaptation than a literal translation—which would have made little sense.

20.3. *He who does not understand words is incapable of under-standing men:* as we have seen, the meaning and function of language is one of the great themes in Confucian thought; it is thus by a singularly befitting accident that the *Analects* should end on this observation. As a modern echo to the final statement of the Master, I shall take leave of my patient reader with this warning by A. E. Housman: "This planet is largely inhabited by parrots, and it is easy to disguise folly by giving it a fine name. Those who live and move and have their being in the world of words and not of things, and employ language less as a vehicle than as a substitute for thought, are readily duped."

PINYIN / WADE-GILES
CONVERSIONS
FOR CHINESE NAMES

Pinyin—Wade-Giles

Ai —— Ai
Anhui —— Anhui
Ao —— Ao
ban —— pan
Bi —— Pi
Bi Gan —— Pi Kan
Bi Xi —— Pi Hsi
bing —— ping
Bo —— Po
Boniu —— Po-niu
Boyi —— Po-yi
Boyu —— Po-yü
bu —— pu
bu ru —— pu ju
Bu Shang —— Pu Shang
Cai —— Ts'ai
Chai —— Ch'ai
Chan —— Ch'an
Changju —— Ch'ang-chü
Chen —— Ch'en
Chen Gang —— Ch'en Kang
Chen Heng —— Ch'en Heng

Pinyin—Wade-Giles

Chen Sibai —— Ch'en Ssu-pai
Chen Xuwu —— Ch'en Hsü-wu
Chen Ziqin —— Ch'en Tzu-ch'in
Cheng —— Ch'eng
Chengpu —— Ch'eng-p'u
Chu —— Ch'u
Cui Zhu —— Ts'ui Chu
dang zhou —— tang chou
Daxiang —— Ta-hsiang
de —— te
Ding —— Ting
Dongmeng —— Tung-meng
Dougou Wutiu —— Tou-kou Wu-t'u
dushu ren —— tu-shu jen
er shun —— erh shun
fan —— fan
Fan Chi —— Fan Ch'ih
Fang —— Fang
Fangshu —— Fang-shu
fei —— fei
Gan —— Kan

Gao Chai —— Kao Ch'ai
Gao Yao —— Kao Yao
Gaozong —— Kao-tsung
ge —— ke
Geng —— Keng
gong —— kung
Gongbo Liao —— Kung-po Liao
Gongming Jia —— Kung-ming Chia
Gongshan Furao —— Kung-shan Fu-jao
Gongshu Wenzi —— Kung-shu Wen-tzu
Gongsun Chao —— Kung-sun Ch'ao
Gongsun Qiao —— Kung-sun Ch'iao
Gongxi Chi —— Kung-hsi Ch'ih
Gongye Chang —— Kung-yeh Ch'ang
gu —— ku
guan —— kuan
Guan Zhong —— Kuan Chung
guishen —— kui-shen
Guo Songtao ——Kuo Sung-t'ao
hai —— hai
Han Feizi —— Han Fei-tzu
Henan —— Honan
hu —— hu
Huan —— Huan
Huainan zi —— *Huai-nan tzu*
Huxiang —— Hu-hsiang
Ji —— Chi
ji ru zai —— chi ju tsai
Ji Sun —— Chi Sun
Ji Wen —— Chi Wen
Ji Zicheng —— Chi Tzu-ch'eng
Ji Ziran —— Chi Tzu-jan
Jian —— Chien
Jieni —— Chieh-ni

Jieyu —— Chieh-yü
Jin —— Chin
Jing —— Ching
Jiu —— Chiu
Jufu —— Chü-fu
junzi —— chün-tzu
junzi daozhe san —— chün-tzu tao-che san
junzi ye —— chün-tzu yeh
Kang —— K'ang
ke qin —— k'e-ch'in
Kong —— K'ong
Kong Decheng —— K'ung Te-ch'eng
Kong Li —— K'ung Li
Kong Yu —— K'ung Yü
Kuang —— K'uang
kuang juan —— k'uang chüan
Lao —— Lao
Lao Zi —— Lao Tzu
Li —— Li
Liao —— Liao
Lin Fang —— Lin Fang
Lin Shu —— Lin Shu
Ling —— Ling
liu yi —— liu yi
Liuxia Hui —— Liu-hsia Hui
Lu —— Lu
Lu Xun —— Lu Hsün
Lunyu li ji chu yanwen di ceyi —— *Lun-yü* li chi ch'u yen-wen ti ts'e-yi
Mao Zedong —— Mao Tse-tung
Mao Zishui —— Mao Tzu-shui
Meng —— Meng
Meng Gongchuo —— Meng Kung-ch'uo
Meng Wu —— Meng Wu
Meng Yi —— Meng Yi
Meng Zhice —— Meng Chih-ts'e

Meng Zhifan —— Meng Chih-fan

Meng Zhuang —— Meng Chuang

Mengjing —— Meng-ching

Mian ——Mien

min ke shi you zhi, bu ke shi zhi
zhi —— min k'e shih yu chih,
pu k'e shih chih chih

Min Ziqian —— Ming Tzu-ch'ien

Nan Rong —— Nan Jung

Nangong Kuo —— Nankung K'uo

Nanzi —— Nan-tzu

Ningwu —— Ning-wu

Peng —— P'eng

Pi Chen —— P'i Ch'en

Pian —— P'ien

pifu —— p'i-fu

Pingqiu —— P'ing-ch'iu

Qi —— Ch'i

Qian Mu —— Ch'ien Mu

Qidiao Kai —— Ch'i-tiao K'ai

Qin —— Ch'in

Qinghua Xuebao —— *Ch'ing-hua
Hsüeh-pao*

Qu Boyu —— Ch'ü Po-yü

Que —— Ch'üeh

Ran Boniu —— Jan Po-niu

Ran Qiu —— Jan Ch'iu

Ran Yong —— Jan Yung

rang —— jang

ren —— jen

renxing —— jen-hsing

ru —— ju

Ru Bei —— Ju Pei

san gui —— san kui

san ren xing —— san jen hsing

Shandong —— Shantung

Shang —— Shang

Shang ren hu? Bu wen ma ——
Shang jen hu? Pu wen ma

Shao Hu —— Shao Hu

Shao nan —— Shao-nan

Shaolian —— Shao-lien

She —— She

Shen —— Shen

Shen Cheng —— Shen Ch'eng

Shen Dang —— Shen Tang

Shen Zhuliang —— Shen Chu-liang

sheng —— sheng

shi —— shih

Shi ji —— *Shih-chi*

Shi Shu —— Shih Shu

Shi Yu —— Shih Yü

shu —— shu

Shuqi —— Shu-ch'i

Shun —— Shun

shuo —— shuo

Shusun Wushu —— Shu-sun Wushu

si wu xie —— ssu wu hsieh

sibai —— ssu-pai

sikou —— ssu-k'ou

Sima Qian —— Ssu-ma Ch'ien

Sima Niu —— Ssu-ma Niu

Song —— Sung

Tai —— T'ai

Taibo —— T'ai-po

Tang —— T'ang

Tantai Mieming —— T'an-t'ai
Mieh-ming

Teng —— T'eng

Wangsun Jia —— Wang sun Chia

Wei —— Wei

weiqi —— wei-ch'i

Weisheng Gao —— Wei-sheng Kao

Weisheng Mu —— Wei-sheng Mu

Wen —— Wen

wenzhang —— wen-chang

Wu —— Wu

wu ri san xing —— wu jih san
hsing

Wucheng —— Wu-ch'eng

Wuma Qi ——Wu-ma Ch'i

Xi —— Hsi

Xia —— Hsia

xiao —— hsiao

Xiang —— Hsiang

xiangqi —— hsiang-ch'i

Xin guancha —— *Hsin Kuan-ch'a*

xingcha —— hsing-ch'a

Xue —— Hsüeh

Xun Zi —— Hsün-tzu

Yan Fu —— Yen Fu

Yan Hui —— Yen Hui

Yan Lu   Yen Lu

Yan Yan —— Yen Yen

Yan Ying —— Yen Ying

Yang —— Yang

Yang Bojun —— Yang Po-chün

Yang Huo —— Yang Huo

Yao —— Yao

yeyi —— yeh-yi

Yi —— Yi

yi se —— yi se

yiduan —— yi-tuan

Yin —— Yin

yong —— yung

You —— Yu

You Ruo —— Yu Jo

Yu —— Yü

Yuan Rang —— Yuan Jang

Yuan Xian —— Yuan Hsien

Yuzhong —— Yü-chung

zai —— tsai

Zai Yu —— Tsai Yü

Zang Sunchen —— Tsang Sun-ch'en

Zang Wuzhong —— Tsang Wu-chung

Zeng Dian —— Tseng Tien

Zeng Shen —— Tseng Shen

Zhan guo ce —— *Chan kuo ts'e*

Zhan Huo —— Chan Huo

Zhan Ji —— Chan Chi

Zhao —— Chao

Zheng —— Cheng

Zheng He —— Cheng Ho

Zhi —— Chih

zhong —— chung

Zhongmou —— Chungmou

zhongren yishang —— chung-jen yi-shang

Zhou —— Chou

Zhou nan —— *Chou nan*

Zhou Ren —— Chou Jen

Zhouxin —— Chou-hsin

Zhu Xi —— Chu Hsi

Zhuan —— Chuan

Zhuang Zi —— Chuang Tzu

Zhuanyu —— Chuan-yü

Zhuzhang —— Chu-chang

Zichan —— Tzu-ch'an

Zifu Jingbo —— Tzu-fu Ching-po

Zigao —— Tzu-kao

Zigong —— Tzu-kung

Zijian —— Tzu-chien

Zilu —— Tzu-lu

Ziniu —— Tzu-niu

Ziqin —— Tzu-ch'in

Zisang Bosi —— Tzu-chang Po-ssu

Ziwen —— Tzu-wen

Zixi —— Tzu-hsi

Zixia —— Tzu-hsia

Ziyou —— Tzu-yu

Zizhang —— Tzu-chang

zong —— tsung

Zou —— Tsou

Zuo zhuan —— *Tso chuan*

Zuoqiu Ming —— Tso-ch'iu Ming

INDEX

Persons, places, titles, concepts and topics (references to the translation are given in roman; references to the notes are in italics).